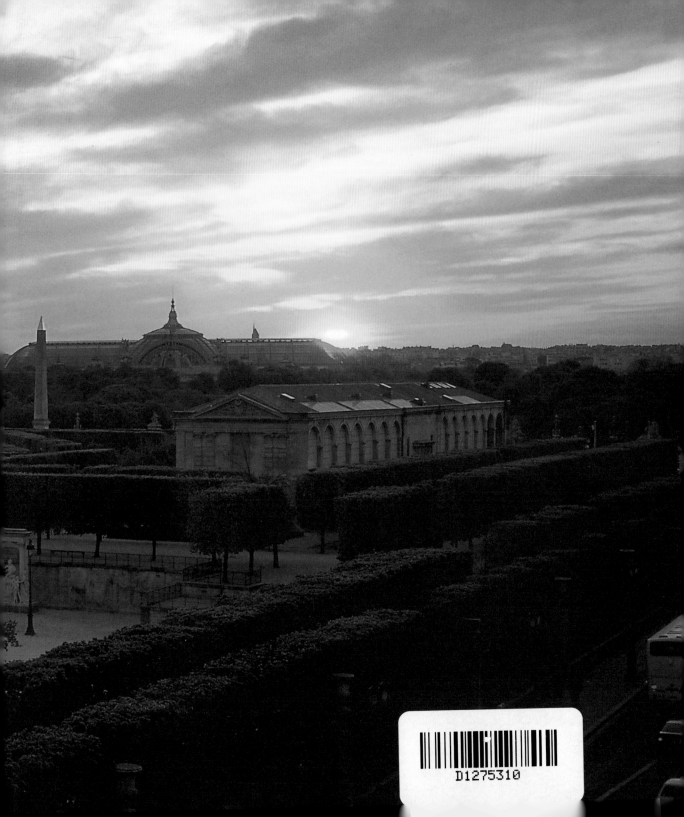
D1275310

THE *Paris*

NEIGHBORHOOD COOKBOOK

First American edition published in 2008 by

INTERLINK BOOKS
An imprint of Interlink Publishing Group, Inc.
46 Crosby Street, Northampton, Massachusetts 01060
www.interlinkbooks.com

Copyright © 2008 Natur och Kultur Publishers, Nygren & Nygren AB and David Loftus Ltd
English translation copyright © 2008 New Holland Publishers (UK) Ltd
American edition copyright © 2008 Interlink Publishing
Packaged by Nygren & Nygren AB
www.nygrenochnygren.se

All rights reserved. No part of this publication may be reproduced, stored in a retrieval system, or transmitted in any form or by any means, electronic, mechanical, photocopying, recording or otherwise, without prior written permission of the publishers and copyright holders.

ISBN: 978-1-56656-723-7

PUBLISHER: *Magnus Nygren*
RECIPES AND FOOD STYLING: *Danyel Couet*
PHOTOGRAPHS AND COLLAGES: *David Loftus*
DESIGN: *Lobby Design*
COVER DESIGN: *Juliana Spear*
TEXT: *Joan Botey*
EDITOR: *Ebba Svennung*
RECIPE EDITOR: *Anita Maurer*
AMERICANIZATION: *Lynne Saner*
PARIS GUIDE: *Marie-Cécile Destandau*
TRANSLATOR: *B.J. Epstein*

PRINTED AND BOUND IN CHINA

All recipes are for 4 people, unless otherwise stated.

Thanks to Johanna A. Zetterlund and Sonja Blaus at Maison de la France/French Tourist Bureau in Sweden for help planning the photography in Paris.

To request our 40-page full-color catalog, please call us toll-free at 1-800-238-LINK, visit our website at www.interlinkbooks.com, or send us an e-mail: info@interlinkbooks.com

THE *Paris*

NEIGHBORHOOD COOKBOOK

DANYEL COUET'S GUIDE TO THE CITY'S ETHNIC CUISINE

DANYEL COUET

PHOTOGRAPHY BY DAVID LOFTUS

Interlink Books

An imprint of Interlink Publishing Group, Inc.
Northampton, Massachusetts

Hicksville Public Library
169 Jerusalem Avenue
Hicksville, NY 11801

In Montmartre is Au Lapin Agile, *which was Paris' first cabaret.*

641.59
C

CONTENTS

"Come with me so I can show you my Paris."

"NO ONE CAN FRY AN EGG LIKE HE CAN," said the world's most famous chef, Paul Bocuse, when he wanted to praise his almost as famous colleague Paul Haeberlin. Like most major chefs, he sees the important things in the simple, and thus the artistry of perfectly frying an egg.

But Monsieur Bocuse cannot have tried my grandmother's fried eggs. Unfortunately. They were fantastic, just like everything else that left her stove. Her kitchen in Paris was the foundation of my lifelong, and sometimes stormy, love for simple, straightforward French food. Here, the onions gave sweetness to the best of all onion soups while lentils, asparagus, and flavorful sausages were all treated equally lovingly. And the fries! There were no better fries than Grandma's.

When I dared to let go of Grandma's apron and the French kitchen, I went on outings with my father. It's easy to do in a metropolis like Paris. A trip on the metro opened a whole new world to me. Just a few stations from our home in Montparnasse, and suddenly all of the world's different tastes were offered.

Of course, many of my new discoveries still concerned France. The classic foods of bistros and brasseries, seafood from the Atlantic coast, dishes from Provence full of aromatic herbs… Around the rue du Bac, I got a taste for freshly made hot chocolate and madeleines, macaroons, marmalades, and delicious baked goods.

Carefully, curiously, and quickly I bit into the globe and its kitchens, tasting yams, *injera*, and plantains in the African 18th arrondissement. After stepping off the metro at Temple, couscous and strong sweet tea in small glasses became favorites to frequently return to. And on the small streets in the Marais, shops with kugel and pastrami and restaurants with baba ghanoush and karp helped me discover Jewish food, ruled by dietary laws. My first real Peking duck—made following all the rules of the art at a simple restaurant in the 13th arrondissement's lively Asian quarter—made me a permanent fan. But I was still passionate about Swedish food too. Despite my adventures, I always longed for my mother's blood pudding, meatballs, and Baltic herring.

After these first steps into the world of food, a trip back to my roots in Paris has also, to a great extent, been a trip back to what formed me as a chef and a person.

Come with me so I can show you my Paris, and therefore also the world, the way I think it tastes. Take a trip through my streets. It's a journey from Tangiers to Lyon, over Hanoi, with stops in Jerusalem's old city as well as Nice.

Bienvenue à Paris!

THE AFRICAN QUARTER

That Africa and the Caribbean meet in one and the same Parisian quarter is not so strange, historically speaking. The markets in La Goutte d'Or are thus a wonderful mixture of familiar and unfamiliar products. If you want to get to know yams or stinkfish, do it here.

FRENCH, WITH THE UNMISTAKABLE ACCENT from "the islands," momentarily drowns out the noisy clucking. The voice belongs to a woman in magnificent, colorful clothes who, like others in the shop, comes from either West Africa or what the French call *outre mer*, "the other side of the sea," islands in the world's warmer regions that still belong to France.

The clucking from the caged hens soon refills the little shop in the middle of La Goutte d'Or, Paris' lively African quarter. The scene is fascinating. Your first thought is that these birds are soon to end their days as fresh products, but our guide, who is in the know, whispers that they are actually sacrificial chickens.

Slowly strolling down the market on rue Dejean quickly triggers the taste buds. The street runs through blocks past their prime, where doors hang at angles and the balconies, which often lean dubiously from the dusty façades, are filled with flowers as well as rubbish.

But the market stands are anything but poor; in big, indiscriminate piles, there are products from Senegal, Haiti, Cameroon, and Ghana. Many of them are completely unfamiliar to me. A packet of fantastic fresh yellow dates is a nice food souvenir that does not feel too foreign.

But if you visit the Maison d'Afrique on rue Dou-deauville, you should introduce yourself to the exciting world of tastes from south of the Sahara and the Caribbean, where many sub-Saharan Africans made their lives after falling victim to the slave trade. My own taste experiences were broadened after I wandered around these stands and looked in shops to see what ends up in saucepans in East and West Africa. It was after a visit here that I began to truly appreciate the Ethiopian bread injera. It is not just a fantastic complement to aromatic dishes from the Horn of Africa, but it also serves as a plate and utensils.

Look for the carob that often finds its way into food when West Africans cook. It is the seed from the St. John's Bread tree and it has a pleasant, slightly chocolatey tone. In the form of flour or syrup, carob leaves its mark on a number of different dishes. Also look out for the range of beans, as there are many kinds to cook with. Look more closely at the vegetable okra, or the frequently used yams – a white sweet potato that after boiling becomes a starchy base for spicy, filling dishes. Not to mention the mountains of plantains, the cans of palm oil, and the coriander seeds in large jute sacks...

And dare to hover over the stinkfish, a dried and salted cod that, despite its name, is everyday food in the Caribbean.

ASSIETTE DE CHIPS
Mixed African chips

1 CASSAVA
1 BLUE CONGO POTATO
1 PLANTAIN
1 YAM
OIL for frying

SPICE SALT
1 TSP GROUND CUMIN
1 TSP GROUND CINNAMON
1 TBSP CORIANDER
1 TBSP GROUND BARBERRY
2 TBSP SEA SALT

1. Peel and slice all the ingredients as thinly as possible.
2. Heat the oil to 320°F (160°C) and fry the thin slices until golden brown.
   Drain on paper towels.
3. Blend all the ingredients for the spice salt together. Salt the chips with the
   spice salt and serve as snacks or as a side dish with meat.

BOULETTES DE YAM

Yam fritters from Ghana

1 LB YAMS, peeled and chopped into thick pieces

2 TBSP SHALLOT, finely chopped

2 HABANERO CHILIES, seeded and finely chopped

3 TBSP CUBED TOMATOES, seeded

1 TBSP SCALLION, finely chopped

1 GARLIC CLOVE, crushed

1 EGG, lightly beaten

CORN FLOUR, for dusting

CORN OIL, for frying

SALT AND BLACK PEPPER

1. Boil the yams in salted water until tender. Drain and mash the yams.
2. Add the shallot, chilies, tomatoes, scallions, garlic, and the beaten egg to the yams. Mix well and add salt and pepper to taste.
3. Shape the dough into balls and roll them in corn flour.
4. Heat the oil to 350°F (180°C). Fry the balls until golden brown. Drain on paper towels. Serve on their own or with fish.

LOUP DE MER MBOGO

Sea bass with spices from Cameroon

2 SEA BASS, gutted and cut in 4 slices

1 SHALLOT, finely chopped

4 PLUM TOMATOES, finely chopped

5 TBSP MARINADE CAMERUN, see recipe below

2 ¼ C FISH STOCK

2 OZ ÉBÈNE SAUCE, available in Asian or other ethnic stores

2 TSP FRESH THYME

1 HABANERO CHILI, seeded and finely chopped

2 BAY LEAVES

2 TBSP LIME JUICE

CORN OIL, for frying

SALT

1. Heat a frying pan and fry the fish over high heat in corn oil until the surface is golden brown. Place on a dish and set aside.
2. Fry the onion in oil without letting it color. Add the tomatoes and simmer over low heat for 5 minutes. Add the marinade camerun, stock, ébène sauce, thyme leaves, chili, and bay leaves. Boil the sauce to a thick consistency. Season with salt and lime juice.
3. Warm the fish in the oven at 400°F (200°C) for 2–3 minutes. Serve with rice, yams, or a salad.

MARINADE CAMERUN

2 C CORN OIL

3 SHALLOTS, chopped

¾ C GRATED GINGER

3 TSP INDIAN PEPPER, ground

7 OZ PARSLEY, chopped

1 GARLIC CLOVE

2 CHICKEN STOCK CUBES

1 TBSP SALT

1 HABANERO CHILI, seeded and chopped

Place all the ingredients in a food processor and mix for at least 10 minutes to a smooth paste. Store in a jar with a tight-fitting lid in the refrigerator.

☞ *I found ébène sauce on one of rue Dejean's cross-streets, in a little shop that was more like a pharmacy than a food store. The sauce includes pink peppercorns and can be successfully used in stews.*

MORUE AUX ÉPICES DE TANZANIE

Spice~fried cod with coconut, chili, and lemon

1 LB COD FILETS

CORN FLOUR, for dusting

PALM OIL, for frying

SPICE MIXTURE

1 TSP GARLIC POWDER

1 TSP CINNAMON

1 TSP CORIANDER

1 TSP DRIED THYME

1 TSP PAPRIKA

1 TSP GROUND BLACK PEPPER

PINCH OF CAYENNE PEPPER

SAUCE

2 TBSP BUTTER

1 SHALLOT, finely chopped

1 GARLIC CLOVE, finely chopped

3 ½ OZ FRESH SPINACH

2 TBSP PARSLEY, chopped

2 TBSP CILANTRO, chopped

1 ¼ C COCONUT MILK

1 TBSP LEMON JUICE

SALT

1. Blend all the ingredients for the spice mixture in a spice or coffee grinder.
2. Separate the fish into portion-sized pieces and dust all over with the spice mixture. Place it in the refrigerator for at least 4 hours before cooking.
3. Warm the butter in a pan over medium heat. Fry the onion and garlic until soft without letting them color. Add the spinach, parsley, and cilantro while stirring. Add the coconut milk and bring to a boil. Remove from the heat. Purée the sauce with a hand blender and season with salt and lemon juice.
4. Heat the palm oil in a pan. Dust the fish with corn flour and fry over high heat until golden brown. Serve the fish with the sauce and with cucumber and lime.

POULET D'AFRIQUE DE L'EST

Roasted chicken with coconut, cilantro, and chili

1 LARGE CHICKEN, 3–4 LB
2 TBSP BUTTER
3 GARLIC CLOVES, crushed
1 TSP GROUND BLACK PEPPER
1 TSP TURMERIC
1 TSP CUMIN
2 TSP CORIANDER
2 TBSP CILANTRO, finely chopped
4 TBSP COCONUT MILK
4 TBSP DRY SHERRY
1 TSP TOMATO PURÉE
SALT
CHILI POWDER

1. Blend all the ingredients except the chicken in a food processor until you have a smooth paste. Season with salt and chili powder.
2. Rub the chicken with the spice paste on top of and under the skin. Let sit in the refrigerator overnight.
3. Place the chicken in a baking dish and cook in the oven at 400°F (210°C) for 25 minutes. Lower the heat to 300°F (150°C) and cook for 25 more minutes. Remove the chicken and let it sit for 5 minutes before serving so it remains juicy. Serve with good rice or oven-baked yams.

The sidewalks overflow with products for sale. Some cardboard boxes are all that is needed to open a store.

PAVÉ DE BŒUF JOLLOF
Roasted sirloin steak with tomato, cinnamon, and chili

1 ¾ LB SIRLOIN STEAK, with the fat

2 TBSP PALM OIL

5 PLUM TOMATOES, finely chopped

1 TBSP TOMATO PURÉE

3 SMALL ONIONS, segmented

2 C CHICKEN STOCK

2 TBSP DRIED SHRIMP, available in Asian stores

1 ¾ C AFRICAN RICE (or regular rice if African rice is not available)

2 GARLIC CLOVES, crushed

1 TSP DRIED THYME

1 CINNAMON STICK, crushed

1 TSP CHILI POWDER

1 TSP TURMERIC

3 ½ OZ BUTTER

2 GREEN CHILIES, seeded and finely chopped

SALT

1. Heat half of the palm oil in a pan and add the tomatoes, tomato purée, and onions. Simmer, covered, for 5 minutes. Add the chicken stock and simmer for 30–40 minutes. Add the shrimp and simmer for 5 more minutes.
2. Wash the rice well and place it in a pan with 1 ¼ c of the stock and 1 ½ c water. Boil for 3 minutes, covered, over high heat. Turn off the heat and let the rice finish cooking in the pan.
3. Rub the sirloin with the garlic, thyme, cinnamon, chili powder, and turmeric. Warm the rest of the palm oil in a pan and brown the beef well.
4. Add a little more stock to the rice and blend in the butter and chopped chili shortly before serving. Add salt to taste and, if desired, more stock so the consistency is light and creamy.
5. Slice the beef and serve with the rice.

SALADE EXOTIQUE À LA NOIX DE COCO

Pineapple and coconut salsa with pomegranate

2 COCONUTS, shell and 3 tbsp grated coconut

1 PINEAPPLE, finely cubed

2 HABANERO CHILIES, seeded and chopped

1 POMEGRANATE, seeds

2 SCALLIONS, thinly sliced

3 TBSP LIME JUICE

1 TBSP PALM OIL

SALT AND BLACK PEPPER

PINEAPPLE LEAVES, shredded, for garnish

1. Halve the coconuts, scrape out the meat, and grate.
2. Mix all the ingredients and add salt and pepper to taste. Place the salsa in the coconut halves. Serve as an accompaniment for grilled food or stews.

BANANES MANDAZI

Banana and vanilla fritters

1 EGG

2 BANANAS, overly ripe

⅔ C MILK

1 VANILLA POD, split and scraped

8 OZ ALL-PURPOSE FLOUR

1 TSP BAKING POWDER

4 TBSP SUGAR

3 TBSP CONFECTIONERS' SUGAR

CORN OIL, for frying

1. Place the egg, bananas, milk, vanilla seeds, flour, baking powder, and sugar in a food processor and mix until smooth. Add a little more milk if the batter gets too thick. Let sit for 10 minutes.

2. Pour the oil into a heavy-based pan and heat to 350°F (180°C). Using a spoon, place balls of batter in the oil and fry until golden-brown. Drain on paper towels. Dust with confectioners' sugar and serve with or without ice cream.

THE ARAB QUARTER

Barbès fires up all the senses: the clatter from the underground and the shouts of the market vendors blend together with the smell of pipes and an endless array of colorful spices. Sit down at a restaurant and collect your impressions over a North African couscous or tagine.

ABOVE OUR HEADS yet another train is on its way towards Barbès-Rochechouart. The steel bridges on their beautiful 32-foot posts shake and sing. For a moment, the noise drowns out the lively trade at the market that extends beneath it along nearly the entire boulevard Barbès.

Once you're in among the stalls, you have to go with the flow. Shoulder to shoulder, at a leisurely pace, you pass tables crammed with artichokes in shades of violet, the ochre-colored spice mix *ras-el-hanout* in coarse paper bags, beautiful cane baskets with all kinds of nuts, and cassette tapes with the latest Algerian pop. Bargaining is something of a sport here. However, it is not always appreciated by the vendors, who, with their slightly abrupt manner, can seem uninterested. And if you look at a product for just a few seconds too long, they may very well claim that you have bought it.

The run-down buildings edging the boulevard and the nearby streets have a worn-out beauty. The walls, in need of a fresh coat of paint, are adorned with decades-old signs and contribute to a patina that would, most likely, be called decay by the quarter's residents. Women in *hijabs* doing their household's daily shopping are seen everywhere and a quick decision about a bunch of crimson radishes can be concluded with a *shukran* as easily as it can with a *merci*. For a moment, you could almost be in a market in Tangiers or Marrakesh.

But this is Paris; or, to be more exact, the 18th arrondissement's heartland, a bit of North Africa in the northern part of France's capital. Of course, Arab influences can be seen throughout the city. France and the Arab world have long been intertwined, not least because of the long periods of colonization.

Today, Arabs are the largest ethnic minority in the country and this is evident in, for example, the magnificent building by Jean Nouvel that houses the *Institut du Monde Arabe,* as well through the small neighborhood shops and all the restaurants with names such as *Chez Omar.*

At a market in Paris or a souk in Marrakesh? Scents, sounds, and the throngs of people make it hard to know for sure.

"For a moment, you can imagine that you are in a market in Tangiers or Marrakesh."

At many of the restaurants, couscous has become a fine art. The small beads of dough are traditionally made of wheat, but sometimes other grains are used. The size varies; the largest are called *berkukes* and the smallest grains are referred to as *seffa* or the more French-sounding *fine*, a clear illustration of the two cultures' influence on each other. In North Africa, couscous is a staple that serves as the base for aromatic accompaniments that can be endlessly varied. Combine the powerful spice paste harissa, *ras-el-hanout*, *merguez*—sausage with a distinctive lamb taste—with chicken with crispy skin and couscous, and you have a dinner to remember.

At the many simple restaurants in Barbès, there are both newly-in-love couples and large families, who bring along both grandma and aunt, for long dinners on the weekends. If you can believe the older men at the next table, the couscous here tastes just like the couscous their mothers used to make at home in Algeria.

Ideally, couscous should be steamed in a *couscoussier*, a type of strainer in which the grains are steamed over pots filled with boiling water. Such an item is of course standard in homes in Barbès, but today they are found in many French homes.

This is also true of the *tagine*, which is best described as a clay casserole dish with a conical cover. Though it is not just the cooking vessel; it's also the name of the casserole that is served in it, and the technique as well. All sorts of goodies can be cooked in a tagine: chicken or lamb is always delicious when cooked with, for example, honey-sweetened tomatoes or bittersweet quince.

A couscoussier and a tagine are often beautiful and useful souvenirs to buy and bring home. They are best bought from the always obliging Aziz, whose shop on rue de Chartres first makes a somewhat chaotic impression but that, after an hour's walk among the stands on the boulevard, becomes a calm oasis. Beans, spices, dried fruit, and beautiful glass jars with whole pickled lemons fill almost every square inch of the little store. Behind the counter, Aziz gives dependable advice about his products and how they should be prepared.

THÉ À LA MENTHE GAZEUS

Carbonated mint tea

4 C MINT TEA
⅔ C SUGAR
4 TSP FRESH MINT
CARBONATE, according to manufacturer's instructions

1. Brew the mint tea.
2. Add the sugar when the tea is hot, then let cool.
3. Pour the tea into a bottle and add carbonate with the help of a sodastream (a home carbonation system). Serve chilled and garnish each glass with a sprig of mint.

☞ *Though we prefer cold drinks in warm weather, in Arab countries people drink hot tea in order to balance the body's warmth.*

TAGINE AU CANARD
Duck tagine with melon

2 DUCK BREASTS

7 OZ PUMPKIN, in segments

¼ HEAD CHINESE CABBAGE, cut in 4 pieces

1 RED ONION, sliced and segmented

2 TBSP OLIVE OIL

½ C GOOD BBQ SAUCE

4 TSP FRESH MINT

4 TSP CILANTRO

4 SCALLIONS, thinly sliced

2 C CUBES OF WATERMELON AND YELLOW HONEYDEW

4 FIGS, quartered

1 POMEGRANATE, seeds

STOCK

1 ONION, finely chopped

1 TBSP GINGER, grated

1 TSP HARISSA

1 CINNAMON STICK

3 CARDAMOM PODS, whole

1 BAY LEAF

2 TBSP BUTTER

½ BOTTLE RED WINE

1 ¼ C CHICKEN STOCK

½ C ORANGE JUICE

SALT AND BLACK PEPPER

1. Start with the stock: fry the onion and spices in butter. Add the red wine and chicken stock and simmer for 30 minutes. Add orange juice, salt, and black pepper to taste.
2. Brown the duck breasts on the skin side. Place in a baking dish and cook in the oven at 250°F (120°C) for 10–12 minutes. Let the breasts sit in a warm place in the kitchen.
3. Boil the pumpkin in salted water until soft. Fry the Chinese cabbage and red onion quickly in the oil.
4. Slice the duck breasts into thin slices. Arrange them with the vegetables and stock. Top with BBQ sauce and garnish with mint, cilantro, scallions, melon, fig, and pomegranate seeds. Serve with couscous.

MERGUEZ
Spicy lamb sausage

1 LB GROUND LAMB
1 LB GROUND BEEF
1 ½ TSP SALT
APPROXIMATELY 7 FT LAMB INTESTINES

SPICE MIX
2 GARLIC CLOVES, crushed
1 TBSP PAPRIKA
1 TSP CUMIN
1 TSP CARAWAY
1 TBSP RAS-EL-HANOUT, see recipe page 48
2 TBSP HARISSA

1. Place all the ingredients for the spice mix in a pan, add ½ c water, and warm without boiling for about 5 minutes. Cool the mix.
2. Blend the meats and work in the salt. Add ¼ c ice-cold water, little by little, until the sausage mixture is smooth and firm. Add the chilled spice mix and blend well.
3. Fill the intestines with the meat and tie off at appropriate lengths. Cut the sausages apart and prick with a needle.
4. Place the sausages on a rack in the refrigerator overnight so they dry slightly and thus do not break when they are fried.
5. Fry the sausages over high heat before serving them.

☞ *In my opinion, merguez is the sausage of all sausages. Cumin and garlic lift the taste of the lamb in an exceptional way.*

MERGUEZ AU CITRON ET HARISSA

Spicy lamb sausage with harissa dressing

4 MERGUEZ SAUSAGES, see recipe page 42
1 BUNCH CILANTRO
SALT AND BLACK PEPPER

HARISSA DRESSING
1 TBSP HARISSA
1 TSP CUMIN
½ TSP CARAWAY
½ TSP CORIANDER
1 GARLIC CLOVE, crushed
½ TSP SALT
¼ C LEMON JUICE
2 TBSP OLIVE OIL

1. Whip the ingredients for the dressing together well.
2. Grill the sausages and slice into smaller pieces. Serve with harissa dressing and cilantro. Roasted or fried potatoes go very well with this.

☞ *Harissa is a North African spice paste made of dried chilies, garlic, and cumin. It can be used successfully in casseroles, soups, and dressings.*

RAS-EL-HANOUT
Arab spice mix

5 BAY LEAVES
4 ROSE BUDS, dried
1 TBSP DRIED THYME
1 TBSP BLACK PEPPERCORNS
½ TSP GROUND MACE
½ TBSP NUTMEG, grated
1 TBSP CLOVES
1 TBSP CORIANDER SEEDS
1 CINNAMON STICK
1 TSP CARDAMOM
1 TBSP CUMIN
1 TSP TURMERIC
1 TSP ANISE SEEDS
1 TBSP DRIED CHILI
1 TBSP GROUND GINGER

Grind all the spices to a powder in a spice or coffee grinder. Store the spice mix in a jar with a tightly-fitting cover. Use in couscous, casseroles, and sauces.

☞ *Ras-el-hanout is a spice mixture that is used in nearly all North African casseroles. I even use it to rub into meat before I grill it. It gives an unbelievably aromatic flavor. Ras-el-hanout is also available ready-made in Middle Eastern stores.*

3 1911 00531 5917

Hicksville Public Library
169 Jerusalem Avenue
Hicksville, NY 11801

Aziz has thousands of items in his charming spice shop on the rue de Chartres.

COUSCOUS RAPIDE
Quick couscous

2 C COUSCOUS
1 TSP PAPRIKA
½ TSP CUMIN
¼ C OLIVE OIL
1 TSP SALT

1. Boil 2 c water, the paprika, cumin, oil, and salt in a large pan.
2. Stir in the couscous, cover, and turn off the heat. Leave to stand for about 8 minutes.
3. Break up the couscous with a fork and serve.

COUSCOUS À L'AGNEAU

Lamb couscous with pumpkin

APPROXIMATELY 2 LB LAMB, shoulder or breast
OLIVE OIL, for frying

STOCK
2 ONIONS, halved
2 GARLIC CLOVES, crushed
5 TOMATOES, scalded
1 TBSP CORIANDER
1 TBSP PAPRIKA
1 TBSP HARISSA
4 CARROTS, halved
2 GREEN CHILIES, halved
2 ZUCCHINIS, thickly sliced
3 RED PEPPERS, seeded and quartered
1 GREEN PEPPER, seeded and quartered
⅔ C PUMPKIN, cut into thick pieces
¾ C CHICKPEAS, soaked for 24 hours
½ C OLIVE OIL
SALT AND BLACK PEPPER

1. Slice the meat into thick pieces and brown well in olive oil. Set aside.
2. Warm the olive oil in a large pan and fry the onion and garlic without letting them color. Add the tomatoes, coriander, paprika, harissa, salt, and pepper. Simmer for 4–5 minutes.
3. Add the browned lamb, carrots, chilis, zucchinis, peppers, pumpkin, and chickpeas.
4. Simmer over low heat for approximately 45 minutes. Add salt and pepper to taste. Serve with couscous.

Tarama
Gehakte Hering
Gehakte Leber
aviar d'aubergines
ge Hongrois & Albanais
Gefilte Fish
Blinis   5.50 €
Pirojki...   5.50
Borsch... MON   7.50
Pikel \Fle...
Latkes...   MECHOUIA
Tchoule... +MECHOUIA
Kreple...   cornichons
         OEUF(CUITE
12H00 A.M

שושנה היטה
MARAIS

BLINIS
chauds tarama

Grand Marnier

21
ANGERIE PATISSERI
Boulan
LE MARAIS
Eglise ST DENIS du
ST SACREMENT
LA LOCANDIERA
BEÏT
YOSS
Triple
Grande
SION
LLIARD
ETTES

THE JEWISH QUARTER

If you're in the mood for strudel or baba ghanoush, this is the neighborhood for you. The Marais is the Jewish people's corner of Paris—therefore, Eastern European food meets North African. But it is also where ancient meets modern, and tradition meets liberalism. The Marais is truly the quarter of contrasts.

THERE IS SOMETHING MYSTICAL about the Marais. Not more than a few blocks from the hordes of tourists in Les Halles and the *flâneurs* outside the modern architectural landmark Centre Pompidou, a whole other world opens up. You automatically slow your steps, peek into the many interesting art galleries, or maybe sit down at a nearby café to people watch for a while. But time can stretch out, with so many characters and personalities to feast your eyes on. *Un café* becomes *un demi de bière*, which then turns into *un verre de vin blanc*, and maybe even dinner. Yes, the Marais is my favorite area in Paris.

Even if the area is slowly transforming into a hip neighborhood, with laid back bars, small, cool shops, and living spaces for all sorts of creative types, all you need to do is turn a corner and feel the quarter completely change character. Before the revolution, the Marais was a fashionable area, which the many spectacular buildings prove. But centuries later homes began to decay, almost becoming slums, and it was not until partway through the 1960s that the area was marked as historical, ending this sad decline. Though the area is, little by little, becoming more chic, the basic character of a charming little city within a pulsing big city still remains.

Above all, it's the big Jewish colony that leaves its stamp. On warm days on rue Pavée, neither Jaffa nor Jerusalem's old city feel very far away. Black Orthodox clothes, *kippas*, and men with big black hats and overcoats are typical sights on the street. And in schoolyards, boys who have not yet had their bar mitzvah play ball in short trousers and well-ironed white shirts, the beginnings of side-locks half-hidden under their caps.

The austere architecture in and around La Place des Vosges serves as a place for both playing and walking.

"The classic salted meat seems to be most tender at Panzer, which is not so strange for a place that calls itself King of Pastrami."

Shops have names like Goldberg and Silberstein. Older ladies can be heard gossiping in Yiddish or Hebrew. Perhaps they're talking about which deli has the best pastrami or *gehackte leber*? The latter is possibly best at Korcarz and the classic salted meat seems to be most tender at Panzer, perhaps unsurprising for a place that calls itself King of Pastrami. After having eaten their famous wares with rye bread, I have to agree.

In the Marais, there are naturally a number of restaurants, bakeries, butchers, and shops that serve Paris' Jewish population. On rue des Hospitalières Saint-Gervais there is Chez Marianne, the restaurant that serves the area's best *mechouia*. From the pavement seating, you have a good view of the commerce in the nearby bookstores, confectioners, and little stores.

Most people are aware that Jewish cooking is strictly regulated by the kosher laws. Ritual slaughter and the prohibition against mixing meat and milk products are two examples of the religious rules for food, preparation, and eating.

But perhaps the Jewish kitchen's most prominent feature is that it has been influenced by the traditions of countries where its people have settled or lived for a long time. That's why at Panzer you find the hearty Eastern European beet soup *borscht* as well as *baba ghanoush*, the roasted eggplant spread that has its roots in the Middle East.

With a jar of pickled vegetables and maybe some pretzels in the bag, a little aimless strolling in the liberal Marais gives you hope. Deeply religious Orthodox Jews meet men in leather clothes on their way to one of the quarter's bars, without any of them raising an eyebrow. Maybe it is the feeling of "live and let live" that best characterizes the Marais.

SALADE DE CAROTTES

Carrot salad

4 CARROTS
½ C CILANTRO
¼ C HARISSA DRESSING, see recipe below
SALT AND BLACK PEPPER

1. Slice the carrots as thinly as possible and place in iced water for about 1 hour.
2. Drain the carrots and then mix with the cilantro. Carefully mix in the harissa dressing, salt, and pepper. Serve as an accompaniment with almost anything.

SAUCE HARISSA

Harissa dressing

1 TBSP HARISSA
1 TSP CUMIN
½ TSP CARAWAY
½ TSP CORIANDER
1 GARLIC CLOVE, crushed
½ TSP SALT
½ C LEMON JUICE
2 TBSP OLIVE OIL

Whip together all the ingredients to make a smooth dressing.

☞ *Harissa dressing also can be served with salads or grilled meat or fish.*

SLATA JIDDA

Tomato and pepper salad

1 GREEN PEPPER, diced

1 RED PEPPER, diced

1 YELLOW PEPPER, diced

4 PLUM TOMATOES, seeded and diced

3 FRESH ONIONS, chopped

½ CUCUMBER, peeled, seeded, and diced

2 LEMONS, grated peel and juice

2 TBSP PARSLEY, chopped

1 TBSP MINT, chopped

2 TBSP OLIVE OIL

SALT AND BLACK PEPPER

1. Mix all the ingredients together. Add salt and pepper to taste.
2. Serve with grilled dishes or as a side dish with couscous.

MECHOUIA
Grilled vegetable salad

2 GREEN PEPPERS
2 RED PEPPERS
2 YELLOW PEPPERS
3 RED CHILIES
2 BEEF TOMATOES, scalded
1 WHOLE FRESH GARLIC
½ TBSP CORIANDER
¼ C LEMON JUICE
½ C OLIVE OIL
SALT

1. Grill the peppers, chilies, and garlic, or place in a hot oven, until their skins are black. Cool them in a bowl covered with plastic wrap. Use a knife to scrape away the burnt skin.
2. Remove seeds from peppers and chop finely, along with the scalded tomatoes and the garlic. Add the coriander and lemon juice and mix well.
3. Place everything in a bowl and cover with oil. Set it in the refrigerator for at least half a day before serving.
4. Serve the mechouia over romaine lettuce leave with grilled meat or fish.

BRICKS À L'ŒUF ET AU THON

Baked tuna with potatoes, eggs, and capers

7 OZ FRESH TUNA

4 EGGS

2 SHEETS OF BRICK DOUGH (a type of filo dough)

2 ONIONS, thinly sliced

2 GARLIC CLOVES, crushed

¼ C PARSLEY

1 TBSP CAPERS

3 POTATOES, boiled and sliced

1 ¼ C OLIVE OIL, for frying

SALT AND BLACK PEPPER

1. Cook the onion and garlic over low heat until soft with 1 tbsp olive oil and ½ c water, until the water has boiled away. Cool.
2. Add the parsley and capers. Add salt and pepper to taste.
3. Separate the brick sheets into 4 half-moons. Distribute the onion mixture and the sliced potatoes among the half-moons.
4. Slice the tuna into 4 equally-sized pieces and place on top of the onion mixture. Break an egg over each. Fold together the sides and roll the bricks together.
5. Warm a frying pan with the oil and fry the bricks until they are golden-brown all the way around. Drain on paper towels. Serve with tomato salad and harissa dressing (see recipe page 60).

CHAKCHOUKA
Vegetable casserole with spicy lamb sausage

6 PLUM TOMATOES, skinned

4 POTATOES, a firm type

½ C OLIVE OIL

2 ONIONS, chopped

4 GARLIC CLOVES, crushed

1 TSP CARAWAY SEEDS, coarsely crushed

3 RED PEPPERS

4 MERGUEZ SAUSAGES, cut into ½ in thick slices (buy ready-made or see recipe page 42)

4 EGGS

SALT AND BLACK PEPPER

1. Quarter the tomatoes and slice the potatoes into pieces 1 x 1 in large. Place in a pan with the oil, onions, garlic, and caraway. Fry for about 5 minutes over low heat. Cover with water and boil until the potatoes are tender.
2. Grill the peppers, or place in a hot oven, until their skins are black. Cool in a bowl covered with plastic wrap. Use a knife to scrape away the burnt skin. Remove the seeds and slice the peppers into smaller pieces.
3. Place the peppers and merguez into the pan with the potatoes and simmer for 10 minutes over low heat, uncovered. Season with salt and pepper.
4. Distribute the chakchouka among 4 individual dishes and break an egg into the middle of each. Bake in the oven at 250°F (120°C) for about 8 minutes. The egg yolk should still be loose when the food is ready. Serve with soft bread.

COUSCOUS AU POISSON
Fish couscous

ABOUT 1 LB WHOLE COD, or another white fish
1 GREEN CHILI, halved
½ TSP SAFFRON STRANDS

STOCK
2 HEADS FROM WHITE FISH
½ C OLIVE OIL
2 ONIONS, halved
2 GARLIC CLOVES, sliced
5 TOMATOES, skinned
1 TBSP CORIANDER
1 TBSP PAPRIKA
1 TBSP HARISSA
4 CARROTS, halved
2 GREEN CHILIES, halved
2 ZUCCHINIS, thickly sliced
3 RED PEPPERS, seeded and quartered
1 GREEN PEPPER, seeded and quartered
⅔ C PUMPKIN, in thick pieces
¾ C CHICKPEAS, soaked for 24 hours
SALT AND BLACK PEPPER

GARNISH
SAFFRON STRANDS
LEMON, shredded peel
GARLIC

1. Place the fish heads in 6 c water in a pan. Simmer over low heat for about 30 minutes. Strain out the heads.
2. Warm the oil in a wide pan and fry the onions and garlic without letting them color. Add the skinned tomatoes, coriander, paprika, harissa, salt, and pepper. Simmer for 4–5 minutes. Add the fish stock, carrots, chilis, zucchinis, peppers, pumpkin, and chickpeas. Simmer over low heat for about 45 minutes. Add salt and pepper to taste.
3. Pour 1 ¾ c of the stock into a low, wide pan together with the green chili and the saffron.
4. Slice the cod into 1 in thick cutlets and add salt and pepper. Let stand for 10 minutes.
5. Place the cutlets in the pan and simmer, covered, over low heat for 6–10 minutes. Garnish with saffron strands, lemon, and garlic. Serve with couscous.

CHREMSLACH

Potato blinis

3 FLOURY POTATOES, peeled
2 OZ BUTTER, room temperature
3 EGG WHITES
CORN OIL, for frying
SALT

1. Boil the potatoes and mash them. Add butter and salt.
2. Whip the egg whites until stiff and add to the mashed potatoes.
3. Heat about ½ in oil in a frying pan. Add circles of batter and fry the blinis until golden-brown on both sides. Serve with whitefish roe and sour cream.

KUGEL DE CAROTTES

Carrot kugel

3 TBSP POTATO FLOUR

8 TBSP WHITE PORT

2 ¼ C CARROTS, grated

3 OZ BROWN SUGAR

8 TBSP DURUM WHEAT FLOUR

1 TSP BAKING POWDER

1 TSP CINNAMON

1 LEMON, grated peel and juice

1 EGG

2 OZ RAISINS

2 OZ DATES, chopped

3 OZ BUTTER, melted

1 DASH SALT

1. Dissolve the potato flour in the wine and then mix in the rest of the ingredients.
2. Pour the mixture into a 7 x 11 in cake pan and bake in the oven at 350°F (180°C) for about 40 minutes until the surface is crispy and golden-brown. Serve warm, with, for example, good ice cream, cream cheese, orange slices, thinly sliced carrot, and mint.

CITRONS CONFITS
Pickled lemons

2 LB SMALL LEMONS
2 RED CHILIES, chopped and crushed in a mortar
3 TBSP SEA SALT

1. Sterilize a large glass jar with a clasp lid by boiling it.
2. Wash the lemons carefully in cold water and cut into wedges.
    Place the lemons and chili in the jar.
3. Boil 4 c water and salt, then let cool for 1 minute. Add the liquid to the jar so it
    covers the lemons. Close the lid and let the jar stand in a cool, dark place for
    3–4 weeks.

☞ *My grandma's interpretation of lemon confits is good both with and in
casseroles and also as an accompaniment for grilled meat or fish.*

MAKROUD
Date~filled semolina fritters

1 LB SEMOLINA
½ C CORN OIL
1 TSP BAKING POWDER
½ TBSP BAKING SODA
1 LB DATES, seeded and finely chopped
3 OZ BLANCHED ALMONDS, finely chopped
3 OZ PISTACHIOS, finely chopped
2 ORANGES, grated peel
CORN OIL, for frying
½ C SUGAR
½ C HONEY

1. Carefully roast the semolina in a dry saucepan. Remove from heat and add the oil. Dilute the baking powder and baking soda in about ¼ c water and add it a little at a time to the semolina until it becomes a dough.
2. Roll out the dough on plastic wrap so that it is 4 x 12 in large and about ½ in thick.
3. Mix together the dates, almonds, pistachios, and orange peel. Place a strip of the mixture on the dough and fold it up with the help of the plastic wrap. Slice it into small pieces. Let sit 1 hour.
4. Heat the oil and fry the dough-bundles until golden-brown. Drain on paper towels.
5. Boil the sugar with a little water and add the honey. Dip the makrouds in the mixture and serve warm.

STRUDEL AUX POMMES ET AUX RAISINS SECS

Strudel with apples and raisins

3 APPLES, peeled and cubed

2 TBSP RAISINS, soaked in 2 tbsp calvados

2 TBSP ALMONDS, blanched, roasted, and chopped

2 TBSP BROWN SUGAR

2 TSP CINNAMON

1 PACKET FILO PASTRY

1 EGG WHITE, for brushing

MELTED BUTTER, for brushing

½ C RAW SUGAR

CONFECTIONERS' SUGAR

1. Mix the apples, raisins, almonds, sugar, and cinnamon.
2. Slice the filo dough into squares approximately 4 x 4 in. Spread a thin layer of the mixture on every square. Brush the edges with egg white and roll into cigar shapes. Brush the rolls with butter and roll in raw sugar.
3. Bake the strudels in the oven at 350°F (180°C) for about 15 minutes until they are golden brown. Dust with confectioners' sugar. Serve warm.

Eglise ST DENIS du ST SACREMENT →

BEÏT   YO

unies a Paris j'espèr
que vous êtes en
bonne santé Vous

ILFORD XP2 SUPER   4 3 4 7

9   ►29A   30   ►30A   31   ►31A   32   ►32A   33

ILFORD XP2 SUPER   4 3 4 7   ILFORD XP2 SUPER

B306875

33A   34   ►34A   35   ►35A   36   ►36A

15

RÉPUBLIQUE FRANÇAISE

Chau
"F"   Sa

RENE LECL
PARIS 9

LES BISTROTS DE PARIS

PARIS — La

PARIS

NEBST EINIGEN

WETTERWALD, BORDEAUX

Propriétaire

J. JANOUEIX

llation Saint-Emilion contrôlée

BISTRO FOOD

Steak fries with bearnaise sauce, onion soup au gratin, quiche lorraine, chocolate mousse... French bistro food has become the restaurant food for the entire western world. No wonder, when it is so simple to make and truly good. And if it is eaten on location in Paris, the charming environment helps, too. Bon appétit!

A 45-minute wait for a table is quite unusual in Paris. Along with a dozen other people, we have patiently waited outside, going back and forth between thinking we will wait in line a little longer or go elsewhere. But I know that a table at Le Bistro d'Henri on rue Princesse is worth waiting for. At the beginning of the 90s, when I worked in Paris, it was here that I often came late at night after my own kitchen closed. The little restaurant with 20 seats is just how you imagine a real French bistro. Here, one chef and one waiter work—the same two as 15 years ago. Well, actually, it turns out that the waiter has a twin brother, so really it's been the three of them.

The checked floor resembles those of many other larger brasseries, where the ceiling height is often impressive, as are the enormous, aged mirrors. The latter are a must at a French establishment of rank, giving one the ability to look around at the entire place even if one's back is facing out. The brass details are polished and the chairs are beautifully worn from the thousands of guests who have passed through over the years. The table's warm red tablecloths are topped with white paper. And it is here that Monsieur David places his hand when he asks what we want to eat. Onion soup, duck confit with lentils, and bitter frisée salad or eggs with mayonnaise, followed by steak fries... Nearly all the classics are on the extensive menu. It is hard to choose. So Monsieur—who despite his gloomy countenance is an expert at recognizing his guests' unuttered wishes—goes to get a bottle of beaujolais for us, so we can decide in peace and quiet what we want most.

A bistro and brasserie wave is making its way around the world. Classic French food served in a classic French environment has become a stylish trend. There are restaurants and bistros in New York,

"A bistro is the type of restaurant my heart beats faster for"

London, and Tokyo that are exact replicas of well established places in Montmartre or on rue du Bac, including welcoming, slightly copperized zinc bars. Possibly the only thing that's missing from these copies are those characters from the neighborhood who, at certain times of the day, sit and gossip over a *pastis*—as they have done for as long as anyone can recall.

It is easy to understand French restaurant culture's triumph over the world, and that of bistros and brasseries in particular. Naturally, it has to do with good food, but also to a large extent, the people, the easy way of socializing, and of course the environment. Together, this is an unbeatable combination where the atmosphere exudes from the walls. The Parisian restaurant has been mythologized and romanticized, in literature and in movies. And sometimes you can almost believe that you see Sartre, Picasso, or Hemingway bent over a *choucroute garnie*.

France has long been a trendsetter for restaurants all around the world. The dominance comes from a bloody upheaval: the French revolution. Chefs who worked for noble and rich families became unemployed when their employers were sent to the guillotine. In order to earn their living, they opened restaurants, which up until then had not been common. Gastronomy quickly spread around Europe from the country that was fashionable in all ways. However, the bistro, with its more rustic and simple environment and food, is based instead on what French mothers, grandmothers, and housekeepers created on the stove. Many of the recipes have been around as long as people remember. Interestingly, the word "bistro" is not French, coming from the Russian word "buistro," which means "fast." It seems that in the 1800s, Russian immigrants—probably fortified by wine and revolutionary plans—sat at restaurants in Paris and shouted "buistro, buistro" in order to get food more quickly. That pretty well sums up the bistro's soul: warm, welcoming, quick, and simple. The type of restaurant my heart beats a little faster for.

Between Paris' thousands of bistros, brasseries, and elegant and celebrated restaurants, there are lots of food places of all kinds. Parisians believe that no one need go hungry or thirsty. And sure enough, it is always crowded at cafés, crêperies, and tea salons.

A ficelle is a longer and more slender baguette.

BAGUETTE FICELLE
Thyme baguette

DAY 1
1 ¼ C WATER
½ OZ FRESH YEAST
1 LB WHEAT BREAD FLOUR
½ OZ SALT

SPICE MIX
2 TBSP THYME LEAVES
2 TBSP SALT FLAKES
2 TBSP BLACK PEPPER, coarsely ground

DAY 2
THE DOUGH FROM DAY 1
2 ½ C COLD WATER
¾ OZ FRESH YEAST
2 LB WHEAT PASTRY FLOUR
1 OZ GOLDEN SYRUP
¾ OZ SALT

1. **Day 1:** Blend all the ingredients except the salt for about 2 minutes. Add the salt and continue to work the dough for 12 minutes in a mixer on low speed.
2. Place the dough in bowl. Cover the bowl with plastic wrap and place it in the refrigerator overnight.
3. **Day 2:** Blend all the ingredients except the salt in a mixer on low speed for 6 minutes. Add the salt and blend 6 more minutes. Let the dough sit for 2 hours.
4. Turn out the dough, which should be loose, and slice it into strips approximately 1 in wide. Place them on a buttered sheet and let rise for 1 ½ hours.
5. Use a spray bottle to spray the bread with water. Sprinkle with the spices. Bake in the oven at 500°F (270°C) until the bread takes on a lovely rich color. Take it out and allow to cool.

☞ *Making a baguette is an art that I, despite a lot of experience, do not possess. Being a baker, unlike being a chef, is not a job but a passion. This recipe is an alternative that has all of the baguette's qualities. The times in the recipe are calculated based on using a mixer, which is always preferable when baking bread.*

BRANDADE
Slow~cooked cod with garlic and thyme

14 OZ COD BELLY, skin- and bone-free
¾ C COARSE SEA SALT
1 ¼ C OLIVE OIL
2 SHALLOTS, finely chopped
7 GARLIC CLOVES, chopped
2 TSP FRESH THYME
2 BAY LEAVES
SALT AND WHITE PEPPER

1. Cover the cod belly with sea salt and let it stand for 1 hour.
2. Warm the oil over medium heat in a saucepan and add the shallots and garlic. Fry for 10 minutes until they are soft but have not colored.
3. Slice the fish into ¾ in cubes. Place the fish, thyme, and bay leaves in with the onions. Set the heat to low and simmer for about 1½ hours.
4. Mix the fish with the oil into a mash. Cool and use to add flavor to dip sauces and potato purées or eat it on its own with good bread.

☞ *Brandade is a kind of fish paste that really should be made of salted, dried fish. A real brandade does not have potatoes, but it is very tasty to blend the fish paste with potatoes and serve it with fried fish or grilled seafood. The secret for making a brandade is that it should cook slowly over low heat; when it is done, you should be able to mix it together like a cream.*

CONSERVE DE THON

Tuna in a jar

14 OZ FRESH TUNA FILLET
2 LEMONS, shredded peel and juice
2 GARLIC CLOVES, crushed
4 TSP FRESH THYME
2 BAY LEAVES
1 TSP BLACK PEPPER, coarsely crushed
1 ¼–1 ¾ C OLIVE OIL
SALT

1. Slice the tuna into 2 equally-sized pieces and salt them well. Cover with plastic wrap and let them sit for 1 hour.
2. Quickly rinse the fish and place the whole pieces in 2 glass jars with clasp lids (about 2 c).
3. Distribute the lemon juice and lemon peel among them. Let sit for about 3 hours in the refrigerator, until the fish has whitened.
4. Distribute the garlic, thyme, bay leaves, and black pepper among the jars. Top off with olive oil and reseal the jars.

☞ *Jarred tuna is often dry and boring. This is a simple recipe I created when I worked at a restaurant in Paris.*

E. Dehillerin at 18 rue Coquillière has delivered kitchen supplies to restaurants and private individuals for almost two hundred years.

POMMES FRITES
French fries

4 LARGE BAKING POTATOES
CORN OIL, for frying
SALT

1. Slice the potatoes into ½ in pieces. Wash them well in cold water to rinse off the extra starch. Drain on paper towels.
2. Heat the oil to 260°F (130°C) in a large, wide saucepan. Place the potatoes in the oil and carefully stir so they do not stick together or break apart. Remove them from the pan after about 10 minutes, when they are coated in a dry film from frying. Spread them out evenly on wax paper. Let them cool.
3. Increase the temperature of the oil to 350°F (180°C) and fry the potatoes until golden brown and very crispy.

☞ *Everyone knows what French fries are. I think there are just as many kinds and qualities as there are countries in the world. I had these French fries at least once a week after school when I was little. But I did not make them myself; it was my beloved grandma who stood in the kitchen then.*

SAUCE BÉARNAISE

Bearnaise sauce

2 EGG YOLKS
2 TBSP TARRAGON VINEGAR
2 C CLARIFIED, MELTED BUTTER
1 TBSP TARRAGON, chopped
1 TBSP PARSLEY, chopped
CAYENNE PEPPER
TABASCO
SALT AND FINELY GROUND WHITE PEPPER

1. Whip the egg yolks, vinegar, and a pinch of salt into a firm and sticky crème in a stainless steel bowl over a double boiler.
2. Add the butter in a thin stream while whipping. Add the tarragon and parsley. Season with salt, pepper, cayenne pepper, and tabasco.

☞ *Unfortunately, most of the bearnaise sauce we eat is ready-made in a jar, frozen, or powdered. Sure, I agree, easy is good. According to a bunch of 200-year-old old men, a classic bearnaise should be boiled down for at least twelve hours, but I dare to contradict them and say that it is actually simpler than that.*

THON À LA NIÇOISE

Tuna salad

1 ½ LB TUNA, sliced into 4 portions

3 ½ OZ GREEN BEANS, lightly boiled in salted water

2 PLUM TOMATOES

8 CHERRY TOMATOES

8 SARDINE FILLETS

4 BABY ARTICHOKES, boiled

8 BABY CARROTS, boiled

4 FRENCH BEANS, boiled in salted water

½ C NIÇOISE OLIVES

2 TBSP RED WINE VINEGAR

1 GARLIC CLOVE, crushed

¼ C OLIVE OIL, good quality

4 SLICES WHITE BREAD, cubed and fried in olive oil

4 EGGS, boiled for 6 minutes and halved

SPINACH LEAVES, to garnish

BASIL, to garnish

PARSLEY, to garnish

SALT AND BLACK PEPPER

1. Salt and pepper the tuna and fry for about 1 minute on each side in a hot pan without any fat. Cool in the refrigerator.
2. Separate the green beans lengthways and slice the tomatoes into thick pieces. Separate each sardine into 4 pieces, halve the artichokes, separate the carrots, and slice the French beans into ¾ in pieces. Mix together all the vegetables, sardines, and olives, and season with salt and pepper.
3. Mix together the vinegar, garlic, and oil. Add salt and pepper. Pour the vinaigrette over the vegetables. Thinly slice the tuna and distribute it on the salad along with the croutons and egg halves. Garnish with spinach, basil, and parsley.

QUICHE LORRAINE
Quiche with bacon and leek

1 LEEK, thinly sliced

2 TBSP BUTTER

½ C DRY WHITE WINE

5 OZ SMOKED BACON, diced

5 OZ MATURE CHEESE, such as Gruyère, grated

4 EGGS

¾ C MILK

¾ C WHIPPING CREAM

PINCH OF GROUND WHITE PEPPER

PINCH OF GROUND NUTMEG

SALT

PASTRY

1 ¼ C FLOUR

PINCH OF SALT

3 ½ OZ BUTTER, sliced in small pieces

1. Place the flour, salt, and butter for the dough in a food processor. Mix until grainy. Add 2–3 tbsp water and quickly mix again. Flatten out the dough and wrap it in plastic wrap. Let it sit in the refrigerator for about 30 minutes.
2. Roll out the dough to discs that cover both the bottom and the sides of four individual 4 in pie plates. Place the dough in the plates and prick with a fork. Cover the sides with aluminium foil. Pre-bake the pastry shells in the oven at 400°F (200°C) for about 10 minutes. Remove the foil.
3. Place the leek in a saucepan together with the butter and wine. Simmer for 30 minutes, until the leek is completely soft.
4. Remove any rind from the bacon. Cut off the fat and set the meat aside. Distribute the leek, bacon fat, and cheese among the pastry shells.
5. Whip together the eggs, milk, and cream. Season with salt, pepper, and nutmeg. Pour the egg mixture into the pastry shells. Bake the tarts in the oven at 400°F (200°C) for 7–10 minutes.
6. Slice the bacon into thin pieces and fry in a hot pan until crispy. Sprinkle the bacon over the quiches. Serve with spinach salad.

"Fine old menus — and a thousand other things — can be found at the flea market by Porte de Clignancourt."

CHÈVRE CHAUD
Baked goat's cheese with honey

1 SMALL BAGUETTE

7 OZ GOAT'S CHEESE, preferably Sainte Maure

½ C ORANGE FLOWER HONEY

1 ORANGE, juice and grated peel

1 TSP TARRAGON, chopped

1 TSP PARSLEY, chopped

1 TSP BASIL, chopped

1 TSP BLACK PEPPER, crushed

FRISÉE LETTUCE, ripped into small pieces

1. Slice the baguette and cheese into slices ½ in thick
   and place the cheese on top of the bread.
2. Mix the honey with the orange juice and orange peel,
   tarragon, parsley, basil, and pepper.
3. Place the bread and cheese rounds on a tray and
   bake in the oven until slightly golden brown.
4. Drizzle the honey mixture over them and garnish with the frisée.

SOUPE À L'OIGNON

Onion soup au gratin with thyme

2 TBSP BUTTER

3 SHALLOTS, thinly sliced

2 RED ONIONS, thinly sliced

2 FRESH ONIONS, thinly sliced

2 GARLIC CLOVES, roughly chopped

1 TSP SUGAR

3 C CHICKEN STOCK

1 ¾ C DRY WHITE WINE

2 BAY LEAVES

1 TSP DRIED THYME

2 TBSP OLIVE OIL

4 SLICES LIGHT COUNTRY BREAD

3 ½ OZ GRUYÈRE CHEESE, coarsely grated

SALT AND BLACK PEPPER

1. Melt the butter in a pan and fry all the onions and garlic until soft, without letting them color (about 5–10 minutes). Stir and add the sugar, stock, wine, bay leaves, and thyme. Simmer for 40 minutes. Season with salt and pepper.
2. Drizzle some oil on the bread slices and bake them in the oven at 525°F (275°C) until lightly golden. Leave the oven on.
3. Pour the soup into four ovenproof soup bowls. Top with the bread slices and a handful of cheese. Bake in the oven at 525°F (275°C) for 5–10 minutes.

COQUILLES ST-JACQUES GRATINÉES

Baked scallops

4 SCALLOPS, in shell
2 TOMATOES, cubes
1 GARLIC CLOVE, crushed
1 TSP TARRAGON, chopped
1 TSP CHERVIL, chopped
1 TSP PARSLEY, chopped
1 TBSP LEMON JUICE
2 TBSP OLIVE OIL
1 EGG YOLK
¼ C WHIPPING CREAM, whipped
SALT AND BLACK PEPPER

1. Remove the scallop shells. Remove the membranes and roe. Add salt and pepper to the scallops and place them back in their shells. Sprinkle the tomato cubes over them.
2. Mix the garlic, tarragon, chervil, parsley, lemon juice, and oil. Season with salt and pepper. Place a tablespoon of the spice oil on each scallop.
3. Stir the egg yolk and add the whipped cream. Place a spoonful of cream over each scallop and bake in the oven at 475°F (250°C) for about 5 minutes.

BOUILLABAISSE
Fish and seafood stew

1 LOBSTER, IN PIECES WITH THE SHELL, boiled

1 LB BLUE MUSSELS

5 SHELLS FROM LOBSTER HEADS, crushed

7 OZ HALIBUT, in 4 pieces

1 WHOLE PIKEPERCH AT 1 ½ LB, cut into 4 thick pieces

ABOUT 7 OZ BONES, skin and trimmings from white fish

2 TBSP OLIVE OIL

1 SHALLOT, thickly chopped

4 GARLIC CLOVES, chopped

1 RED CHILI, halved

½ RED PEPPER, roasted until black, cut into pieces

½ FENNEL, thickly sliced

1½ TBSP TOMATO PURÉE

PINCH OF SAFFRON

5 RIPE TOMATOES, thickly sliced

14 OZ CAN CHOPPED TOMATOES

2 C FISH STOCK

½ C WHITE WINE

2 TSP FRESH THYME

2 BAY LEAVES

2 STALKS OF PARSLEY

1 LEMON, juice

1 ORANGE, juice

SALT AND WHITE PEPPER

ROUILLE

¼ C PIMENTO

(roasted Spanish pepper in a jar)

1 POTATO, boiled

2 GARLIC CLOVES, roasted

1 TBSP BASIL, chopped

½ C OLIVE OIL

1 TBSP LEMON JUICE

TABASCO

SALT AND BLACK PEPPER

1. Fry the lobster heads in hot oil for about 15 minutes. Add the fish bones, skin, and trimmings, shallot, garlic, chili, pepper, and fennel, and fry for 5 more minutes.
2. Add the tomato purée and fry for 5 more minutes.
3. Add the saffron, tomatoes, fish stock, and white wine and boil for 5 minutes. Add enough water to cover everything, along with the thyme, bay leaves, and parsley stalks. Simmer for 30 minutes.
4. Strain the soup and boil the liquid until it is reduced by half. Season with the lemon juice, orange juice, salt, and pepper.
5. Season the fish with salt and pepper. Fry it in oil and finish it with a little freshly-squeezed lemon juice.
6. To make the rouille, place the pimento, potato, garlic, and basil in a food processor and mix until smooth.
7. Add olive oil a drop at a time. Season with salt, pepper, lemon juice, tabasco, and a little soup.
8. Place the blue mussels in the soup right before serving. Boil for 4 minutes. Put the fish and seafood on 5 plates and top with fennel fronds. Serve with the cold rouille.

This quick-to-make and simple stew is suitable for both parties and everyday and is so good that no one will want to leave the table until it is finished.

AGNEAU PROVENÇAL
Roast lamb with goat cheese and bean salad

1 ¼ LB LAMB LOIN

1 TSP FRESH THYME LEAVES

1 TBSP COARSELY CHOPPED PARSLEY

1 TSP ROSEMARY

2 PLUM TOMATOES

2 TBSP SMALL WHITE BEANS, boiled

½ HEAD OF BROCCOLI, boiled and cut into florets

1 FENNEL BULB, boiled and cut into pieces

1 SHALLOT, thinly sliced

10 GREEN BEANS, boiled and sliced

¼ C LEMON JUICE

¼ C OLIVE OIL

3 ½ OZ GOAT'S CHEESE

SALT AND BLACK PEPPER

1. Slice the lamb into portion-sized pieces, season with salt and pepper, and brown in olive oil in a frying pan. Sprinkle the thyme, parsley, and rosemary over the meat and baste with the oil in the pan. Roast the meat in the oven at 250°F (120°C) for approximately 10 minutes.
2. Dip the tomatoes first in boiling water and then cold, and peel off the skin. Slice each tomato into 8 pieces and place in a large bowl with the rest of the vegetables and beans.
3. Add lemon juice, olive oil, salt, and black pepper to taste.
4. Distribute the cold vegetable mixture among plates, top with the meat, and crumble goat's cheese on top.

☞ *If you want to get extra taste from the lamb, it works well to marinate the meat in red wine and herbs overnight.*

BŒUF BOURGUIGNON
Bœuf bourguignon

5 OZ SMOKED BACON

2 LB BEEF FLANK

2 CARROTS

2 TBSP BUTTER

2 SHALLOTS, chopped

5 GARLIC CLOVES, chopped

1 BOTTLE BURGUNDY WINE

3 BAY LEAVES

5 TSP FRESH THYME

2 ¼ C VEAL GRAVY, or 3 tbsp crumbled beef
    stock cube boiled with 2 ¼ C water

SALT AND BLACK PEPPER

ACCOMPANIMENTS

12 SMALL ONIONS, peeled

BUTTER, for frying

1 TSP SUGAR

3 TBSP LEMON JUICE

1 ½ TBSP OLIVE OIL

7 OZ FRESH MUSHROOMS, sliced and sautéed

4 ASPARAGUS SPEARS, lightly boiled in
    salted water

8 BABY CARROTS, boiled

3 TBSP PARSLEY, chopped

SALT AND BLACK PEPPER

1. Cut the rind and fat off the bacon and set aside. Cut the bacon meat into small cubes and brown in a frying pan. Set aside.
2. Cut the beef into 2 in cubes and pat dry with paper towel. Season with salt and pepper. Slice the carrots into 1 in pieces.
3. Fry the bacon rind in a pan. Add butter if the meat is not very fatty. Add the beef when the rind has begun to get a little color. Brown the beef on all sides. Add the carrots, shallots, and garlic when the beef is browned. Continue to fry for a couple more minutes.
4. Pour in the wine. Stir and scrape the bottom of the pan so that you loosen any meat juices. Add the bay leaves and thyme. Stir again and add enough gravy so that it easily covers the meat. Simmer, covered, over low heat for about 2 hours. Occasionally, skim off the fat with a spoon.
5. Brown the onions in butter in a frying pan until they are nicely colored. Season with salt, pepper, and sugar. Continue to fry until the sugar turns golden brown. Place on a dish.
6. Mix the lemon juice and olive oil in a bowl and add salt and pepper. Add the sautéed mushroom slices.
7. Slice the bread into ½ in cubes and fry in butter until golden brown. Drain the croutons on paper towels.
8. Lift out the meat and carrots with a slotted spoon and place them in a bowl. Boil the sauce over medium heat until the consistency is syrupy.
9. Return the meat to the pan. Top with asparagus, baby carrots, mushrooms, croutons, bacon, and parsley just before serving. Serve with potato purée or linguini.

MOUSSE AU CHOCOLAT

Chocolate mousse

9 OZ DARK CHOCOLATE, 70% cocoa, finely chopped
1 EGG YOLK
2 TBSP ARMAGNAC OR GRAND MARNIER
2 C WHIPPING CREAM, lightly whipped
MINT LEAVES, to garnish

1. Melt the chocolate in a double boiler. Add the egg yolk and brandy.
2. Remove the pan from the heat and mix in half of the cream with a spatula. Stir together until smooth. Add the rest of the cream. Cover the bowl with plastic wrap and put in the refrigerator for at least 3 hours before serving.
3. Serve the chocolate mousse with raspberries, whipped cream, or grated dark and white chocolate. Garnish with mint leaves.

FLAN
Vanilla flan

8–10 PEOPLE

4 C MILK
1 VANILLA BEAN, seeds scraped out
6 EGGS
2 ¼ C SUGAR

1. Boil the milk and vanilla seeds, then remove from heat. Allow to cool for
   10 minutes. Break the eggs and stir into the vanilla milk. Strain.
2. Pour ⅔ c water into a pan, add the sugar, and boil for about 15 minutes until it turns
   to a golden brown caramel. Do not stir during that time.
3. Stop the cooking process by adding ½ c water. Distribute the caramel among
   8–10 individual 3 in ramekins. Let harden for 5 minutes. Distribute the milk and egg
   mixture among the dishes.
4. Pour boiling water into a deep baking tray or roasting dish. Place the individual dishes
   in the water and bake in the oven at 325°F (170°C) for about 15 minutes, until the
   crème has hardened. Remove from the oven and cool in the refrigerator.
5. Overturn the puddings and serve.

☞ *This is my grandmother's fantastic recipe. The pudding itself has neither
sugar nor cream; the caramel contains all the sweetness.*

CRÊPES AU CITRON

Crêpes with lemon syrup

3 EGGS
1 VANILLA BEAN, seeds scraped out
PINCH OF SALT
ABOUT 1 ¼ C FLOUR
3 TBSP CORN OIL
ABOUT 2 ¾ C MILK
CORN OIL, for frying

FOR THE LEMON SYRUP
½ C SUGAR
2 OZ BUTTER
5 TBSP LEMON JUICE

1. Place the eggs, vanilla seeds, and salt in a bowl. Add the flour a little at a time while whipping, until it becomes a smooth, thick batter. Add the oil and stir in.
2. Add the milk so the batter becomes thin like pancake batter.
3. Brush the frying pan with oil before each crêpe and cook over medium heat.
4. Boil the sugar and butter to a syrup in a saucepan. Add the lemon juice and simmer for 3 minutes. Allow to cool and serve with the crêpes.

☞ *The secret to good and really, really thin crêpes is a well-oiled cast iron or teflon pan that is oiled before each crêpe.*

TRUFFES AU CHOCOLAT
Chocolate truffles

7 OZ DARK CHOCOLATE, 70% cocoa

½ C WHIPPING CREAM

1 VANILLA BEAN, seeds scraped out

1 TSP GRATED ORANGE PEEL

2 TBSP GRAND MARNIER

2 TBSP BUTTER, room temperature

PINCH OF SALT

1 ½ TBSP DARK COCOA POWDER

1. Chop the chocolate and place it in a bowl.
2. Boil the cream with the vanilla and orange peel. Pour the cream over the chocolate. Stir until smooth.
3. Stir in the Grand Marnier. Stir in the butter a little at a time. Add the salt and pour the mixture into a dish or rectangular plate. Allow to cool and harden in the refrigerator.
4. Slice the chocolate into squares and roll them in cocoa powder. Place in a container with wax paper between the layers. Cover and store in the refrigerator.

Paris' own vineyard is in Montmartre, on the slope behind Sacré Cœur.

MONSIEUR LE COMTE   BIBLIOTHÈQUE   MADEMOISELLE

PARIS — Panorama d

MENU

JOURS DE FRANCE

MATCH

P

AU MARCHÉ

MARKETS AND STREET FOOD

Though Paris can be proud of what may be the world's largest selection of restaurants, sometimes you may prefer to eat lunch outdoors for the opportunity to taste all the delicious treats you can't resist at the markets and gourmet shops.

OFFHAND, I CANNOT THINK of anything better than a really well-filled baguette eaten in a park on a sunny day. All due respect to artistic food on a beautifully set table, elegant settings, and attentive service, but there are times when no advanced cooking can be compared to a quickly organized picnic.

Naturally, a picnic does not have to do with just the food, but also with the environment (there is nothing like eating outdoors!) and the good friends who have been tempted along. All told, it's an unbeatable combination.

A filling baguette, or a *ficelle*, as the extra slender type is called, is fast and simple to prepare. But often, a picnic does not require more than a few wise purchases, which, of course, is easy to do in Paris where nearly every neighborhood has its own bakery, butcher, and wine store. The danger with buying picnic food is simply that you buy too much.

First to the cheese shop: Paris is a stinking heaven for cheese-lovers. A fully ripe camembert, a lively roquefort, and characterful chèvre go straight in the shopping basket. Don't miss *les traiteurs*, the gourmet shops, which can be found everywhere. A substantial piece of paté with the right accompaniments, a good ham from Savoyen, and a tasty sausage from Auvergne are musts. You must also go to the bakery. A proper sourdough bread should be bought, and maybe a baguette or two. And a couple of *pains au chocolat*.

Certainly, many are tempted by the seafood hawker's impressive selection. A dozen belon oyster from Normandy are fantastic with shallot vinaigrette. The classic wooden keg in which they are sold is also beautiful in itself and just right to embellish a French picnic. Just don't forget the oyster knife...

Keep off the grass in Le Jardin des Tuileries! A picnic with Jessica on one of the garden's many walls.

"The danger with buying picnic food is simply that you can buy too much."

Or the corkscrew—that's right, wine! Nothing too advanced. A light red, or even better, a nice rosé from Tavel. Lunch can take a while—even stretch out until dinner.

A good way of working up your appetite and gathering all your purchases from one place is, naturally, to go to a marketplace. Despite the name, it has been a long time since the classic Les Halles was the right place for this kind of shopping. But there are many exciting markets all around Paris. A great example is the Marché Richard Lenoir in the 11th arrondissement, near La Bastille. Besides all the artfully arranged pyramids of tomatoes, the rows of sausages, and the shoals of fish on ice—and the freshest asparagus, brought to the city early in the morning—the opportunity to inhale the atmosphere is reason enough to come. Noisy market madames, old men bargaining, and the smell of fresh fruit and vegetables bring you very close to the stomach of Paris.

Wherever I travel in the world, my professional curiosity takes me to the area's wholesale markets. In Paris, I always take the opportunity to go to Rungis, in the north of the city. Naturally, it is not just chefs who draw inspiration from wandering in the gigantic hangars filled with goodies. It isn't every day that you can see artichokes that were harvested just four hours earlier or can breathe in the scent of the best cheeses whether from cow, goat, or sheep's milk.

Now all that's left is to choose the picnic site, which can be pretty hard in a city with fantastic parks and river banks with excellent spots for observing tourist boats and crowds. If I am on boulevard Richard Lenoir, I might take a blanket to the Parc de la Villette a bit north, or sit on a bench along the equally well-trafficked and beautiful Canal Saint-Martin. If you set your sights on Le Jardin des Tuileries—the amazing park between Place de la Concorde and the Louvre—keep off the grass! I didn't. Immediately a guard on a bicycle came by and directed us to the park's special picnic area. Pretty boring. But one of the Tuileries' many walls works just as well for a successful outing with food.

OLIVES DEMI SÈCHES AU VINAIGRE
Dried olives in vinegar

7 OZ SUN-DRIED BLACK OLIVES

2 TBSP PARSLEY, chopped

3 TBSP SUN-DRIED TOMATO, chopped

2 GARLIC CLOVES, crushed

1 RED CHILI, thinly sliced

Mix all the ingredients. Store in a jar with a tight-fitting lid in the refrigerator.

OLIVES VERTES AU PIMENT
Marinated green olives

7 OZ LARGE GREEN OLIVES

½ RED PEPPER, roasted and peeled

1 TBSP DRIED CHILI FLAKES

1 TSP SUGAR

2 TBSP LEMON JUICE

2 GARLIC CLOVES, finely chopped

Mix the pepper, chili flakes, sugar, lemon juice, and garlic in a food processor. Place the olives in the marinade. Store in a jar with a tight-fitting lid in the refrigerator.

OLIVES NIÇOISES
Nice olives

7 OZ NICE OLIVES (small black)

2 SHALLOTS, sliced

⅓ C CHAMPAGNE VINEGAR

¼ C COCKTAIL CAPERS

1 TBSP THYME, fresh

4 BAY LEAVES

2 TBSP OLIVE OIL, good quality

1 TSP BLACK PEPPER, crushed

1. Place the shallot slices in the vinegar and let stand for about 30 minutes, until they have started to soften.
2. Remove the shallots and mix with the rest of the ingredients.
3. Store in a jar with a tight-fitting lid in the refrigerator.

LE CAMEMBERT
Filled camembert

1 RIPE, CHILLED CAMEMBERT (it should be as soft at the edges as it is inside)
1 DRIED FIG, coarsely chopped
2 DRIED APRICOTS, coarsely chopped
1 TBSP RAISINS
1 TSP CURRANTS
1 TSP CELERY LEAF, chopped

1. Separate the camembert in the middle, like a hamburger bun.
2. Mix the rest of the ingredients together and place on the bottom half of the cheese. Put the other half on top and press together well.
3. Pack the cheese in wax paper and put it in the picnic basket. Bring a good dark bread to eat with it.

L'ARTICHAUT
Wine~cooked artichokes

4 ARTICHOKES
ABOUT ¾ C OLIVE OIL
2 GARLIC CLOVES, crushed
3 TSP FRESH THYME
2 BAY LEAVES
1 TSP BLACK PEPPER, crushed
1 LEMON, halved
2 PLUM TOMATOES, halved
2 FRESH ONIONS
¾ C WHITE WINE
SALT

1. Trim the artichokes until only the hearts are left. Heat the oil in a pan and add the artichokes along with all the other ingredients except for the wine. Fry for 2–3 minutes, then add the wine and boil for 1 minute.
2. Add enough water to cover the artichokes. Weigh it down so the artichokes are always under water. Simmer for 10–15 minutes, depending on the size. Allow to cool in the liquid.
3. Serve the artichokes warm or cold. The strained stock works well in sauces or soups.

LES SARDINES
Pickled sardines

ABOUT 10 OZ SARDINE FILLETS, or baltic herring fillets
1 ¼ C LEMON JUICE
1 TBSP VINEGAR
2 TBSP SALT

MARINADE
1 LEMON, grated zest
2 TSP FRESH THYME
1 TSP BLACK PEPPER, crushed
3 BAY LEAVES
2 GARLIC CLOVES, thinly sliced
OLIVE OIL

1. Stir together the lemon juice, vinegar, and salt. Add the sardines and marinate for 30–45 minutes, until the flesh is almost completely white.
2. Strain off the liquid and layer the sardines in a jar together with the lemon zest, thyme leaves, pepper, bay leaves, and garlic. Top with oil so that all is covered. These are good with freshly baked country bread on picnics.

At Marché Richard Lenoir, there are good stinky cheeses, oysters and fresh vegetables—but also crafts, clothes, and tools.

With all due respect to oysters, they can taste good with something on the side, too. Here are some simple recipes for accompaniments.

CONCOMBRE ET CITRON
Cucumber and lemon juice

½ CUCUMBER, peeled and finely grated
4 SCALLIONS, finely chopped
3 LEMONS, juice, and the grated peel of 2
SALT

Mix all the ingredients. Add salt to taste.

ÉCHALOTES MARINÉES
Sour shallots

4 BANANA SHALLOTS
¾ C CHAMPAGNE VINEGAR

Thinly slice the shallots and place them in the vinegar. Let marinade for 2 hours before serving.

CITRON ET PIMENT VERT
Lemon and green chili

3 LEMONS, finely chopped without peel and membranes, and grated peel of 1
4 GREEN CHILIES, seeded and finely chopped
1 TBSP OLIVE OIL
SALT

Mix all the ingredients. Add salt to taste.

LE HOMARD

Boiled lobster

2 LIVE LOBSTERS, about 1 lb each
1 ½ OZ SALT PER 4 CUPS WATER
½ HEAD CELERY

1. Fill a tall pan with salted water and boil it with the celery.
2. Discard any rubber bands from the lobsters' claws. Place the lobsters in the water and boil for 5 minutes. Remove from the heat. If you want to eat them warm, leave the lobsters in the water for just 5 minutes. Let them cool in the liquid if you prefer them cold.

☞ *Often, you are told to boil lobsters way too long, which means that the meat gets tough and dull. There are many ways to make lobster so that it is tender and juicy. You can salt and boil it in water or simmer it in oil over low heat. You can grill it in its shell or boil it according to this recipe. The celery strengthens the seafood taste.*

FICELLE GOURMANDE
Luxury baguette

1 BAGUETTE FICELLE, see recipe page 89

2 TBSP CREAM CHEESE

2 TBSP OLIVE OIL

2 ROASTED PEPPERS, available ready-made

4 SLICES AIR-DRIED HAM

2 OZ FOIE GRAS TERRINE, sliced with a cheese slicer

1 SCALLION, thinly sliced

2 TSP FRESH BASIL

SALT AND BLACK PEPPER

1. Split the baguette. Mix the cream cheese with the olive oil and spread on the bread.
2. Add the peppers, ham, foie gras, onion, and basil. Season with salt and pepper. Place the other half of the baguette on top and wrap tightly in wax paper to keep the filling together. Slice the bread into portion-sized pieces and place it in the picnic basket.

L'ÉPAULE D'AGNEAU
Marinated lamb shoulder

1 LAMB SHOULDER

SEA SALT

5 SUN-DRIED TOMATOES, roughly chopped

4 GARLIC CLOVES, crushed

10 TSP FRESH THYME

1 TSP FRESH ROSEMARY

1 ORANGE, shredded peel

1 LEMON, shredded peel

1 TSP BLACK PEPPER, crushed

1 CINNAMON STICK, crushed

¼ C OLIVE OIL

1. Rub sea salt into the lamb shoulder and let stand at room temperature for an hour, until the salt begins to melt.

2. Brush off the salt from the shoulder. Mix the rest of the ingredients in a bowl. Make small cuts in the meat and fill with some of the spice mixture. Also rub the spice mixture into the meat.

3. Place the meat on a dish and cover with plastic wrap. Place somewhere cool and leave to marinate for 1 day before cooking it. Barbecue, grill, or roast the lamb shoulder.

"With Place de la Concorde on one side and the Louvre on the other, the magnificent Jardin des Tuileries is one of Paris' foremost meeting places."

LA RHUBARBE
Rhubarb with roasted almonds

10 RHUBARB STALKS, peeled
¾ C SUGAR
2 SLICES MADIERA CAKE, or similar cake, cut into small cubes
4 TBSP ALMONDS, roasted and grated
4 TSP FRESH MINT, chopped

1. Wash the rhubarb stalks and cut into pieces 6 in long. Place in a long baking dish or tray and sprinkle the sugar on top. Bake in the oven at 400°F (200°C) for about 7 minutes, until the rhubarb is soft. Remove from the oven and let cool.
2. Place the cake cubes on a baking tray. Bake them in the oven at 400°F (200°C) for about 7 minutes, until golden brown.
3. Place the rhubarb on a dish and pour the juice from the pan over it. Sprinkle the almonds and roasted cake cubes on top. Sprinkle with fresh mint and serve with lightly whipped cream or ice cream.

☞ *Rhubarb is one of my favorites. Along with the spring's first stalks comes a feeling of summer. This is a simple summer dessert.*

SAINT-
MICHEL

THE GREEK QUARTER

If the choice of holiday destination is between Paris and the Greek islands, for me it's easy to choose. In the area around Saint-Michel, there is an authentic bit of Greece, complete with charming rickety chairs, lamb cutlets with lemon—and tourists. The only thing really missing is the glitter from the Mediterranean.

THERE IS FOOD THAT just exudes comfort; you know what I mean. It's that simple, unpretentious food that can be so marvelously good. The kind that you recognize, have eaten many times, and that doesn't surprise you with its taste.

Real comfort food is the sort you fall in love with from the first moment, at the first bite.

Food from the Greek school of cooking fits the bill perfectly. Olives, oil, aromatic thyme and oregano, and lots of lemon set the tone. The method of preparation is often very simple: a pair of substantial lamb cutlets or super fresh, almost jumping, fish, or squid that is put on the grill and served directly with nothing more than lemon.

Also, comfort food is often filled with memories, and when it comes to Greek food, for many people that means sunny days and warm nights on holiday. A tasty grouping of meze dishes is one of the high points. Some nicely rolled dolmades and feta cheese together with a couple of well made, cool dips such as *tzatziki*, hummus and eggplant caviar invite you to sit for a long time and chat. My thoughts travel back many years to my island-hopping days. Amorgos, Paros, Crete… every new place in the Greek islands created new food memories.

But if you are in Paris, you do not need to go very far south to experience this Greece. In the area around rue Saint-Séverin and rue de la Huchette, in the 5th arrondissement, you can find a little Athens or the Dodecanese in the diaspora.

Here, there are almost as many tourists as there are in the eastern Mediterranean. There's something of a holiday feel on the streets. If you stay, you'll soon find yourself sitting with a menu in your hand on a rickety chair with a braided seat—one of the very determined and noisy hawkers makes sure of that. Many Parisians take the underground to Saint-Michel late at night to end a really fun evening on the town with a good-sized pita with *gyros*—the epitome of comfort food.

F2.8 1/320 CENT H AFS F2.5 80mm

KODAK PORTRA 400UC   51

AUBERGINE MELIZANO
Grilled eggplant dip

4 EGGPLANTS

2 PLUM TOMATOES

2 GREEN CHILIES

1 C OLIVE OIL

3 GARLIC CLOVES, crushed

2 TBSP PARSLEY, finely chopped

⅓ C LEMON JUICE

SEA SALT AND BLACK PEPPER

1. Grill the eggplants on a charcoal grill or in the oven at 425°F (225°C) for 30 minutes. Turn them occasionally. Grill the tomatoes and chilies in the same way, but just until the skins have blackened. Remove the vegetables from the grill and cool for 5 minutes in a bowl.

2. Remove the skins from the vegetables and process them quickly in a food processor. Add the olive oil, garlic, parsley, and lemon juice. Add salt and pepper to taste.

☞ *This is a wonderful buffet dish that goes well with grilled food.*

TZATZIKI

Cucumber salad with yogurt and lemon

½ C GREEK YOGURT
½ GARLIC CLOVE, crushed
3 TBSP LEMON JUICE
1 CUCUMBER, peeled and cut into thick pieces
3–4 TSP FRESH OREGANO
OLIVE OIL
SALT AND BLACK PEPPER

Mix the yogurt with the garlic and lemon juice. Add salt and pepper to taste. Blend in the cucumber and garnish with oregano and olive oil.

 *This cooling cucumber salad goes especially well with grilled meat.*

DOLMADAKIA
Grape leaf dolmades with feta, tomato, and olives

1 JAR GRAPE LEAVES, available in ethnic food stores

2 BEEF TOMATOES, chopped and drained in a colander

2 TBSP OLIVE OIL

2 TBSP FETA CHEESE, crumbled

2 TBSP PINE NUTS, chopped

3 TBSP BLACK OLIVES, chopped

2 SHALLOTS, finely chopped

1 GREEN CHILI, finely chopped

½ C OMELETTE (made with 1 egg and chopped)

SALT AND BLACK PEPPER

SHERRY VINEGAR

1. Mix together all the ingredients except for the grape leaves. Add salt, black pepper, and vinegar to taste.
2. Place the filling on the grape leaves and roll together. Serve with a Greek salad.

CALAMARES FRITS
Calamari with black aioli

4 CALAMARI, cleaned and cut in rings ¼ in thick

1 GARLIC CLOVE, crushed

2 TBSP BASIL, finely chopped

1 TSP DRIED OREGANO

1 LEMON, grated peel and juice

1 TSP BAKING POWDER

¼ C FLOUR

¼ C CORN FLOUR

ABOUT 1 C MINERAL WATER

CORN OIL, for frying

CORN FLOUR, for dusting

AIOLI

1 EGG YOLK

½ GARLIC CLOVE, crushed

1–2 TBSP LEMON JUICE

1 ¾ C OLIVE OIL, good quality

1 TSP SQUID INK, available at fish markets

SALT

TABASCO

1. Mix the garlic with the herbs, lemon peel, and 1 tbsp lemon juice. Carefully add the squid rings and marinate for 1–2 hours.
2. Blend together the baking powder, flour, and corn flour. Add the mineral water a little at a time until the consistency is thick and lumpy.
3. Heat the oil to 350°F (180°C) in a heavy-based pan. Roll the rings in the corn flour and then dip in the flour batter. Fry the rings until golden-brown. Drain on paper towels.
4. Whip together the egg yolks, garlic, and lemon juice. Add the olive oil in a thin stream while whipping. Add enough ink so the aioli turns completely black. Season with salt, tabasco and, if desired, more lemon juice. Serve with the aioli on the side.

CALAMARES FARCIS
Grilled squid filled with feta and tomato

12 MINI-CALAMARI
½ C FETA CHEESE, crumbled
3 TBSP PARSLEY, chopped
1 TBSP GRATED LEMON PEEL
2 GARLIC CLOVES, crushed
2 TOMATOES, seeded and chopped
SALT AND BLACK PEPPER

TOMATO DRESSING
4 RIPE PLUM TOMATOES, finely chopped
½ GARLIC CLOVE, crushed
¼ C SHERRY VINEGAR
½ C OLIVE OIL, good quality
SALT AND BLACK PEPPER

TOPPING
2 TBSP LAVENDER FLOWERS
1 TSP THYME FLOWERS
1 TSP PARSLEY, chopped

1. Remove the membranes from the squid and wash in cold water. Chop the tentacles and mix with the feta, parsley, lemon peel, garlic, and tomatoes. Season with salt and pepper.
2. Fill the squid bodies with the mixture and thread them on skewers so the filling does not fall out.
3. Blend all the ingredients for the tomato dressing together.
4. Cook the squid under a hot grill. Serve with the tomato dressing, topped with herbs.

POULPE À LA LAVANDE

Octopus stew with lavender

1 OCTOPUS, about 2 lb
1 HEAD FENNEL, sliced
4 SHALLOTS, halved
3 GARLIC CLOVES, thinly sliced
¾ C OLIVE OIL
5 PLUM TOMATOES, quartered
2 ¼ C DRY WHITE WINE
4 BAY LEAVES
1 TSP DRIED OREGANO
1 LEMON, juice
2 LEMONS, halved
4 TSP FRESH OREGANO
2 TBSP LAVENDER FLOWERS
SEA SALT AND BLACK PEPPER

1. Boil the octopus in salted water for 5 minutes, then drain. Slice the octopus into thick pieces.
2. Warm a heavy-based saucepan and fry the shallot and garlic in oil for about 5 minutes. Add the octopus and fry for 5 more minutes. Add 3 c water and the rest of the ingredients except for the lemon, oregano, and lavender. Simmer over low heat for about 30 minutes, and use a fork or cake tester to check when the octopus is tender. Season with lemon juice, salt, and pepper.
3. Garnish with oregano and lavender flowers. Serve with lemon and new potatoes.

Do as many Parisians do: go to Saint-Michel to end the evening with a good-sized pita with gyros.

BROCHETTES DE LOTTE THALASINO
Monkfish skewer with shrimp and squid

1 ⅓ LB MONKFISH FILLET, cut into 1 in cubes

8 MEDIUM SHRIMP, halved

½ SQUID, boiled in salted water for 20 minutes and cut into smaller pieces

2 TBSP MINT, chopped

2 TBSP OREGANO, chopped

2 GARLIC CLOVES, crushed

1 LEMON, grated peel

½ C OLIVE OIL

8 SMALL RED ONIONS

SALT AND BLACK PEPPER

1. Mix together the mint, oregano, garlic, lemon peel, and oil to a marinade. Season with salt and pepper.
2. Layer the monkfish, shrimp, squid, and onions onto a skewer.
3. Brush the marinade on the skewer and let sit in the refrigerator at least 1 hour. Cook under a hot grill until the skewers start to color.

BOULETTES D'AGNEAU

Lamb meatballs with feta

14 OZ GROUND LAMB

1 EGG YOLK

½ C FETA, crumbled, plus extra to serve

1 TSP MARJORAM

1 GARLIC CLOVE, crushed

1 TSP OREGANO, chopped

1 TSP CUMIN

2 OZ BUTTER, for frying

2 TBSP OLIVE OIL, for frying

4 PLUM TOMATOES, grated

¼ C OLIVE OIL

2 TBSP SHERRY VINEGAR

SALT AND BLACK PEPPER

1. Mix the lamb meat, egg yolk, and a little salt to a paste. Add 2 tbsp cold water, the feta, marjoram, garlic, oregano, and cumin. Roll into small meatballs and fry in butter and olive oil.
2. Mix together the tomatoes with ¼ c oil and the vinegar. Season with salt and pepper. Serve with the fried meatballs. Top with crumbled feta and a little oregano.

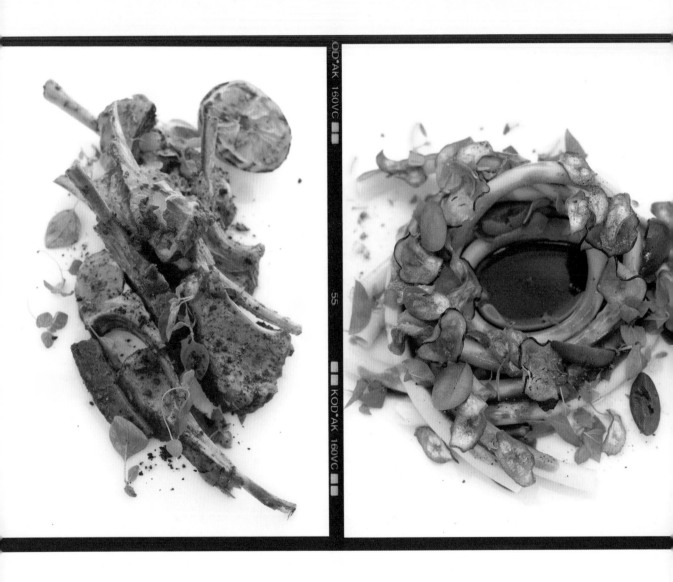

CÔTELETTES D'AGNEAU AUX MACARONIS

Lamb cutlets with long macaroni

2 RACKS OF LAMB

2 GARLIC CLOVES, crushed

1 TBSP LEMON JUICE

1 LEMON, grated peel

1 TBSP OREGANO, finely chopped

1 TBSP PARSLEY, finely chopped

1 TSP LAVENDER FLOWERS, finely chopped

¼ C + 2 TBSP OLIVE OIL

1 ¾ C RED WINE

1 TBSP SHERRY VINEGAR

1 ZUCCHINI, thinly sliced

1 EGGPLANT, thinly sliced

¼ C BLACK OLIVES, stoned and halved

1 LB LONG MACARONI

SALT AND BLACK PEPPER

1. Mix the garlic, lemon juice, lemon peel, oregano, parsley, and lavender with olive oil. Brush the lamb with the marinade. Leave to stand at room temperature for 30 minutes. Season with salt and pepper.
2. Fry the meat on all sides in 1 tbsp oil in a frying pan until it is nicely colored. Then brush on more marinade. Do not wash the pan.
3. Place the meat on a tray and roast in the oven at 250°F (120°C) for about 10 minutes.
4. Pour the red wine into the unwashed pan and boil with all the remaining flavors until one-third of the wine is left. Add the sherry vinegar. Salt the vegetables and fry them in ½ c oil until they are golden brown.
5. Cook the pasta and add to the red wine gravy. Add the rest of the marinade. Slice the cutlets and serve together with the vegetables and pasta.

YAOURT DE BREBIS

Sheep's yogurt with black olives

1 ¼ C GREEK YOGURT
½ C FETA, crumbled
2 TBSP OLIVE OIL
1 GARLIC CLOVE, finely chopped
15 HALF-DRIED BLACK OLIVES, pits removed and coarsely chopped
2 TSP FRESH OREGANO
2 TSP FRESH MARJORAM
SALT AND BLACK PEPPER

1. Blend the yogurt and feta until smooth in a food processor. Add
   1 tbsp olive oil and salt to taste. Place in a bowl.
2. Mix the rest of the olive oil with the garlic and drizzle it over the
   yogurt. Sprinkle the olives over and top with oregano and
   marjoram leaves. Finish with coarsely ground black pepper.

☞ *This yogurt also goes well with strong food or grilled dishes.*

FIGUES FLAMBÉES AU YAOURT

Yogurt crème with flambéed figs

8 FRESH FIGS, halved
2 ¼ C PLAIN YOGURT
1 ¾ C WHIPPING CREAM
⅔ C HONEY
2 TBSP LEMON JUICE
2 TSP GRANULATED GELATIN
1 TBSP BUTTER
4 TBSP RAW SUGAR
1 ORANGE, shredded peel
¼ C OUZO
MINT LEAVES

1. Mix the yogurt with half of the cream.
2. Boil the rest of the cream with the honey and lemon juice. Remove from heat and add the gelatin. Mix together the honey mixture with the yogurt mixture and pour into 8 individual dishes. Allow to set in the refrigerator for at least 2 hours before serving.
3. Heat the butter and sugar in a frying pan until the sugar has turned golden brown. Add the figs, with the cut-side down, along with the orange peel, and cook for 3 minutes. Remove from heat, add the ouzo and quickly ignite. Serve on top of the yogurt crème and garnish with mint leaves.

☞ *Be careful when flambéing. It's nicer to eat a good dessert when no one is injured…*

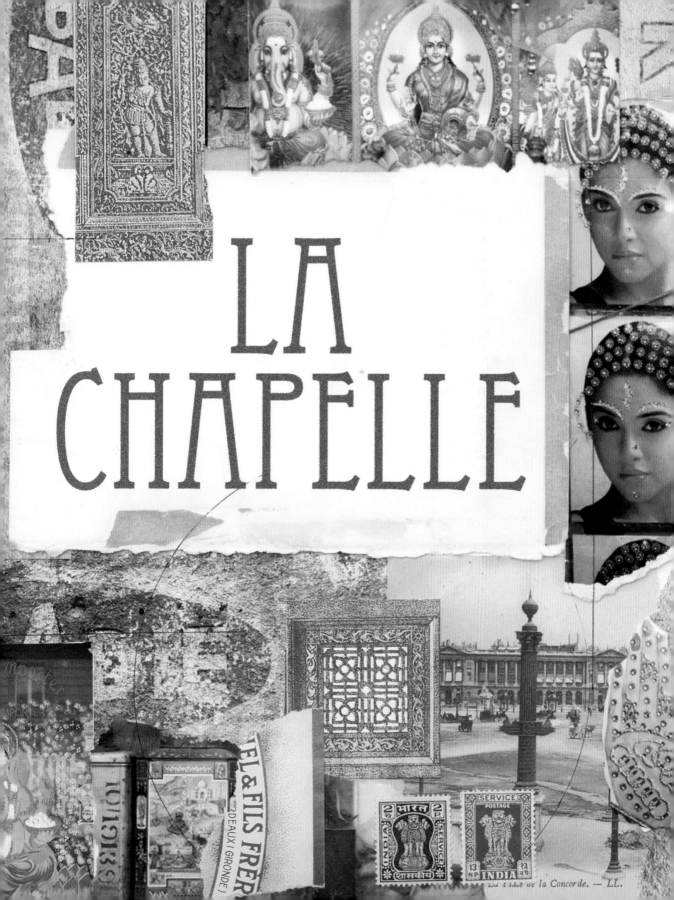

LA
CHAPELLE

THE INDIAN QUARTER

You can of course eat tandoori in Paris, too. Indian food is as common here as in all big cities. But take the chance to try something you aren't familiar with. In La Chapelle, practically all the shops and restaurants are Indian, and the smell of aromatic curry paste lies heavily over the quarter.

MY ROAD TO INDIA goes via rue du Faubourg Saint Denis, which cuts right through the 10th arrondissement. In the area surrounding the La Chapelle metro station, it's more Hindi and Urdu that you hear on the streets rather than French. Beautiful, colorful saris are much more prevalent than sober Chanel, and Sikh gentlemen are seen dashing in and out of the swarm of shops on the hunt for new turbans.

The quarter certainly has many stores connected with food, but inspiration, as is well known, can come from things other than exotic products. In Paris' "Little India," the whole atmosphere—which is so hard to capture and yet is felt in the air—creates a desire to immediately put together a flavorful curry paste, or maybe a really sweet and fruity grapefruit chutney, which complements everything from lamb steaks to fresh grilled fish.

Old posters for Bollywood films, stores filled with Vishnu statues, a gigantic shop with everything—from clothes to pots—that you might need for a big Kashmiri wedding, or suddenly finding a fine little tea cup with its accompanying teapot—all this puts me in the mood for cooking Indian dishes.

To try to summarize India and its multi-faceted and rich food tradition so briefly is clearly taking on too much. India is home to over one billion people. There are 15 main languages spoken throughout the country, and close to a thousand smaller ones. Most of the inhabitants live according to one of the many religious traditions that strongly influence how and what they eat.

With the snowy Himalayas in the north, a tropical south, and all imaginable conditions for cultivation and breeding in between, India boasts a wide variety of cooking styles.

The Indian dishes most of us are familiar with from restaurants here in Europe come from the Punjab area, the tandoori's promised land. And, yes, skewers with lamb or chicken and other dishes cooked in the traditional clay oven are really delicious.

But "Indian" is much more than that—there is a fantastic world of taste to discover. Not least, the many vegetarian dishes are exquisite. As is the quickly baked naan bread, which, together with the clarified butter ghee, can be served as a complement or as a practical utensil for characterful dishes bursting with tamarind, caraway, or innumerable spice mixtures.

PAIN CHAPATI
Chapati bread

14 OZ FINE WHOLE-WHEAT FLOUR
1 ½ TSP SALT
1 TBSP GHEE, available in Asian stores, or clarified butter

1. Mix the flour and salt with 1 c water in a mixer. Add the ghee when the dough has come together. Work the dough for about 7 minutes in a mixer, or 15 minutes by hand.
2. Let the dough sit for 30 minutes.
3. Separate the dough into golfball-sized balls and roll them out until thin. Fry the bread in a hot dry pan until it bubbles up. Turn over and repeat on the other side.
4. Cover the cooked chapatis with a clean towel while you cook the rest. Serve immediately.

PAIN NAAN
Naan bread

⅔ C MILK, warm

2 TSP BROWN SUGAR

2 TSP DRY YEAST

14 OZ ALL-PURPOSE FLOUR

½ TSP SALT

1 TSP BAKING POWDER

2 TBSP CORN OIL

⅔ C PLAIN YOGURT

1 EGG, lightly beaten

1. Pour the warm milk, half of the sugar, and the yeast into a bowl and let stand for 20 minutes.
2. Sift the flour in a big bowl together with the salt and baking powder. Add the other teaspoon of sugar, the yeast mixture, oil, yogurt, and the beaten egg.
3. Knead the dough for 7 minutes in a mixer on low speed, or by hand for about 15 minutes.
4. Grease a bowl with a little oil, place the dough in the bowl, and roll it in the oil. Cover the bowl with plastic wrap or a lid and let the dough rise in a warm place for about 1 hour, until it has doubled in size.
5. Place a tray in the oven and turn up the heat as high as it will go.
6. Separate the dough into golfball-sized balls. Roll them out to a thickness of about ¼ in.
7. Place the dough on the preheated baking tray—do not remove it from the oven. Bake in the hot oven for about 3 minutes or until the breads have swollen and started to color.
8. Cover the finished breads with a towel and serve immediately.

POORI
Fried puffed bread

3 OZ WHOLE-WHEAT FLOUR
1 TSP CORN OIL
PINCH OF SALT
CORN OIL, for frying

1. Place all the ingredients in a mixer, add
   ¼ c water, and run on low speed
   for 7 minutes, or knead by hand for
   15 minutes. Let the dough rest for
   30 minutes.
2. Separate the dough into 12 pieces and roll
   out each one to thin rounds 1/8 in.
3. Heat the oil to 350°F (180°C) in a deep,
   heavy-based pan. Fry the breads until they
   bubble up. Drain them on paper towels.
   Serve with chutney and pickles.

CHUTNEY AU PAMPLEMOUSSE
Grapefruit chutney

1 ½ TBSP CORN OIL

½ TSP BLACK MUSTARD SEEDS

1 TSP WHOLE CUMIN SEEDS

¼ TSP WHOLE ANISE SEEDS

¼ TSP WHOLE FENNEL SEEDS

10 OZ GRAPEFRUIT, without peel or membranes

½ CINNAMON STICK

1 TBSP SUGAR

½ TSP GROUND GINGER

1 TSP SEA SALT

½ TSP CAYENNE PEPPER

1. Heat the oil over medium heat in a frying pan. Add the mustard seeds and as soon as they begin popping, add the cumin, anise seed, and fennel. Roast for about 1 minute.
2. Pour 1 c water in the frying pan and boil over low heat for 10 minutes, until half the liquid is left.
3. Add the rest of the ingredients and simmer for 10 minutes, until the consistency is chutney-like. Allow to cool.
4. Pour the chutney into jars with tight-fitting lids. Store in a cool place.

CHUTNEY À LA MANGUE
Mango chutney

4 UNRIPE MANGOS, peeled and cut into strips

7 OZ SUGAR

¾ C APPLE CIDER VINEGAR

1 TBSP GINGER, grated

4 RED CHILIES, chopped

SALT

8 GREEN CARDAMOM PODS

1 TSP WHOLE ANISE SEEDS

1 TSP FENUGREEK, crushed

1 CINNAMON STICK, crushed

1. Place the strips of mango in a pan together with the sugar, vinegar, ginger, chili, and salt. Mix and simmer for 10 minutes over low heat.
2. Roast the spices in a dry hot pan. Mix them into the mango mixture.
3. Continue simmering until the mango is soft, but not completely mushy. Season with salt and, if desired, more vinegar.
4. Serve the chutney with spicy casseroles or as a snack with poppadoms.

CHOU-FLEUR NEW DELHI
Pickled cauliflower

1 CAULIFLOWER HEAD, broken into florets

3 TBSP CORN OIL

1 TBSP WHOLE MUSTARD SEEDS

4 TBSP CURRY POWDER, see recipe page 226

4 SHALLOTS, quartered

3 GARLIC CLOVES, thinly sliced

ABOUT 1 IN GINGER, thinly sliced

10 GREEN CHILIES, in ¼ in slices

1 ¼ C APPLE CIDER VINEGAR

SALT

1. Heat the oil in a frying pan and fry the cauliflower florets over high heat until they have browned.
2. Add the mustard seeds and curry powder. Fry for 2–3 more minutes over high heat.
3. Place the cauliflower in a bowl, add the rest of the ingredients, and carefully mix. Allow to cool.
4. Store the cauliflower in jars with tight-fitting lids in a cold place. Serve as a spicy accompaniment for meat or fish or with poori, see recipe page 196, and poppadoms.

LENTILLES PUNJAB
Punjabi lentil curry

LENTIL CURRY

3 ½ OZ BLACK LENTILS

3 ½ OZ ORANGE LENTILS

2 TOMATOES, grated

2 GARLIC CLOVES, crushed

1 TBSP GINGER, grated

2 GREEN CHILIES, finely chopped

SALT

TARKA (SPICE MIXTURE)

1 SHALLOT, finely chopped

1 TSP CORN OIL

2 TBSP BUTTER

1 TSP GROUND CUMIN

½ TSP GARAM MASALA, see recipe p. 220

2 GARLIC CLOVES, crushed

½ TSP CHILI POWDER

6 TBSP CHOPPED CILANTRO

1. Pour 3 ⅓ c water in a pan. Add all the ingredients for the curry and simmer for 1 hour over low heat.
2. Fry the shallot in the oil and butter in a frying pan. Add the cumin, garam masala, garlic, and chili powder. Continue frying for 1 minute. Mix the tarka with the lentil curry and add the cilantro. Add salt to taste.

PAIN PERDU ANDA PAV
Salty poor knights of Windsor

4 EGGS, lightly beaten
½ C WHIPPING CREAM
1 ONION, finely chopped
1 GREEN CHILI, finely chopped
1 TSP GARAM MASALA, see recipe page 220
1 TSP GINGER, grated
1 GARLIC CLOVE, crushed
2 TBSP CILANTRO, chopped
SALT
4 SLICES WHITE BREAD
SUNFLOWER OIL, for frying

1. Whip together the eggs, cream, onion, chili, garam masala, ginger, garlic, and cilantro.
2. Add salt to taste.
3. Soak the bread for 1 minute in the batter. Fry the bread slices in oil until golden brown.
4. Serve the bread with fresh mint and curry oil, see recipe page 223.

FLÉTAN AUX ÉPICES
Spice~fried fish

1 ⅓ LB WHITE FISH, such as halibut, flounder, or sea bass, with skin

1 TBSP WHOLE FENNEL SEEDS

1 TSP BLACK MUSTARD SEEDS

1 TSP WHOLE CUMIN SEEDS

1 CINNAMON STICK, crushed

1 TSP TURMERIC

½ TSP GROUND BLACK PEPPER

1 TSP GINGER, grated

1 TSP SALT

2 TBSP CORN OIL

SAUCE

1 TSP BUTTER

1 TBSP CILANTRO, finely chopped

1 GREEN CHILI, finely chopped

¼ C ORANGE JUICE

SALT AND BLACK PEPPER

1. Roast the fennel seeds, mustard seeds, cumin, and cinnamon in a dry hot pan. Allow to cool.
2. Grind the spices to a powder in a spice or coffee grinder. Combine the spice mixture with the turmeric, pepper, ginger, and salt.
3. Slice the fish into portion-sized pieces and rub them with the spice mixture. Warm a frying pan with oil. Fry the fish for about 3 minutes on each side.
4. Lift the fish out of the pan and put in the butter, cilantro, and chili. Fry about 1 minute. Add the orange juice and season with salt and black pepper. Strain the sauce and serve it with the fried fish.

"In the area around the La Chapelle underground station it's Hindi and Urdu that you hear on the streets."

CURRY DE POULET RAPIDE

Fast chicken curry

1 CHICKEN, cut in thick, equally-sized pieces
1 ONION, thinly sliced
2 TBSP CORN OIL
1 TBSP BLACK MUSTARD SEEDS
3 TSP GARLIC, crushed
3 TBSP CURRY PASTE, see recipe page 225
½ C WHIPPING CREAM
½ C YOGURT
1–2 TBSP APPLE CIDER VINEGAR
3–4 TBSP CILANTRO, chopped
SALT AND WHITE PEPPER

1. Fry the onion in the oil in a large pan for 5 minutes without letting it color. Add the mustard seeds and garlic. Fry for 5 more minutes.
2. Season the chicken with salt and pepper and brown on all sides in oil in a separate frying pan.
3. Add the chicken to the onion with the curry paste, cream, yogurt, and ¼ c water. Simmer over low heat for 20 minutes.
4. Season the curry with salt and apple cider vinegar. Finish by sprinkling cilantro over it. Serve with rice.

POPPADUMS AU CURRY
Lamb poppadoms with peach

4 POPPADOMS, available in Asian stores

1 ⅓ LB LAMB LOIN

1 ONION, finely chopped

1 TSP GINGER, grated

2 GARLIC CLOVES, crushed

2 TBSP CURRY PASTE, see recipe page 225

APPLE CIDER VINEGAR

OIL, for frying

SALT AND BLACK PEPPER

FRESH PEACH, cut into chunks

YOGURT

MINT

1. Season the meat with salt and pepper. Brown on all sides in oil in a frying pan. Place the meat in a baking dish and roast in the oven at 250°F (120°C) for about 15 minutes.
2. Fry the onion, ginger, and garlic in oil over low heat until the onion is soft.
3. Add the curry paste and ½ c water. Simmer to a thick consistency. Add salt and apple cider vinegar to taste.
4. Warm the oil to 250°F (180°C) in a heavy-based pot. Fry the bread in the oil.
5. Cut the meat into slices and serve with the poppadoms, sauce, peaches, yogurt, and mint.

PICKLES À LA PÈCHE
Pickled Peaches

2 LB RIPE PEACHES, in segments

2 TBSP FENNEL SEEDS

1 CINNAMON STICK, crushed

1 TBSP ANISE SEEDS

¾ C CHICKPEAS, boiled

5 ½ OZ CURRANTS

3 RED CHILIES, chopped

1 TBSP GINGER, grated

1 LB RAW SUGAR

2 ½ C APPLE CIDER VINEGAR

3 TSP MINT

2 SHALLOTS, sliced and in 4 tbsp apple cider vinegar

SALT

1. Roast the fennel seeds, cinnamon, and anise seed in a hot dry pan. Add everything except the peaches, mint, and shallots. Simmer over low heat for 10 minutes. Allow to cool.
2. Add the peaches, mint, and shallots. Store in a cool place in a jar with a tight-fitting lid. Serve with spicy casseroles or as a snack with poppadoms.

LASSI AU COCO ET AU CITRON VERT

Coconut and lime lassi

1 ¾ C PLAIN YOGURT
¾ C COCONUT MILK
5 TBSP SUGAR
1 TSP GROUND CARDAMOM
1 TSP GROUND CINNAMON
1 TSP GROUND GINGER
20 ICE CUBES
4 LIMES, grated peel and juice
4 TSP MINT LEAVES

1. Blend everything except the mint in a blender or with a handheld mixer.
2. Serve the lassi in tall, chilled glasses with straws. Garnish with mint leaves.

☞ *Lassi can be made sweet or salty. I prefer sweet.*

GARAM MASALA
Indian spice mixture

1 TBSP BLACK CARDAMOM, available in Asian stores, or regular cardamom
1 TBSP BLACK PEPPER
1 TSP CUMIN SEEDS
1 TSP WHOLE CLOVES
⅓ NUTMEG, crushed
1 CINNAMON STICK, whole

1. Heat up a frying pan and quickly roast the spices without fat until they really perfume the air. Put them in a bowl and allow to cool.
2. Grind the spices to a powder in a spice or coffee grinder. Store in a jar with a tight-fitting cover. Use in casseroles and curry dishes.

HUILE AROMATIQUE
Curry oil

½ C SUNFLOWER OIL

1 GARLIC CLOVE, crushed

1 TSP GINGER, grated

1 TBSP CUMIN SEEDS

1 TSP TURMERIC

1 TSP GROUND FENNEL SEEDS

1 TBSP CILANTRO, finely chopped

1 TSP TAMARIND PURÉE, available in Asian stores

1 TSP BLACK MUSTARD SEEDS

1 TSP FENUGREEK, crushed

1. Mix together all the ingredients and warm until it just begins to bubble.
2. Store the oil in a cool place in a jar with a tight-fitting cover.

PÂTE DE CURRY
Curry paste

4 TBSP WHOLE CORIANDER SEEDS
1 TBSP WHOLE BLACK PEPPER
2 TSP WHOLE CUMIN SEEDS
1 TBSP BLACK MUSTARD SEEDS
1 TBSP WHOLE FENNEL SEEDS
10 CURRY LEAVES, dried
1 ONION, finely chopped
3 GARLIC CLOVES, crushed
1 BUNCH FRESH CILANTRO, finely chopped
⅔ C CORN OIL
⅔ C APPLE CIDER VINEGAR
1 TBSP TURMERIC
1 TBSP CAYENNE PEPPER
½ TSP GROUND CARDAMOM
2 TSP GROUND GINGER
2 TSP SALT
2 TSP BROWN SUGAR

1. Put all the spices and the curry leaves in a cool dry pan. Place the pan over high heat. Roast until the spices begin to really perfume the air. Pour the spices into a bowl and let cool.
2. Grind the spices to a powder with a spice or coffee grinder.
3. Fry the onion, garlic, and cilantro in the oil over low heat for about 30 minutes without them letting them color.
4. Add ½ c water, the roasted spices and the rest of the ingredients, and simmer, covered, over the lowest heat for 15 minutes.
5. Pour into jars with tight-fitting covers. Use the paste in casseroles or as an accompaniment.

CURRY EN POUDRE
Curry powder

4 TBSP CORIANDER SEEDS, whole
1 CINNAMON STICK
5 WHOLE CLOVES
1 TBSP WHOLE CUMIN SEEDS
1 TBSP WHOLE CARDAMOM PODS
1 TSP WHOLE BLACK PEPPER
1 TBSP WHOLE FENNEL SEEDS
2 STAR ANISE
10 CURRY LEAVES, dried
1 TBSP DRIED CHILI FLAKES
1 TSP GROUND GINGER
5 TBSP TURMERIC
1 ½ TSP CAYENNE PEPPER
1 TSP BLACK MUSTARD SEEDS
¼ TSP GRATED NUTMEG

1. Roast all the whole spices in a dry hot pan until they begin to really perfume the air. Place in a bowl and let cool.
2. Grind the spices to a powder with a spice or coffee grinder. Add the rest of the spices.

☞ *There are several thousand different curry mixtures. All families have their own variation. I got this recipe from my Indian childhood friend.*

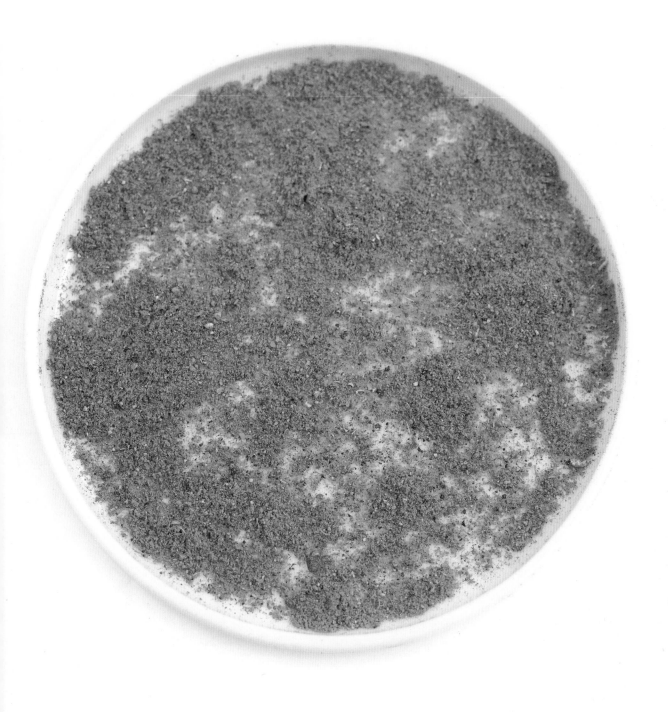

LE
TREIZIÈME

THE ASIAN QUARTER

There is a "Little Asia" in most big cities and Paris is no exception. In the 13th arrondissement, you can find everything from lacquered Peking ducks to crispy Vietnamese spring rolls and countless exciting spice combinations. Few areas can equal the variety of shops and restaurants—they aren't big, but they are many!

WELL WITHIN THE PLASTIC COVERING that creates a shelter outside the storefront, I wait patiently with the others. We are all here on the same errand. Hooked up on display inside the window hangs the reason for our line: Peking ducks with their beautiful, crispy, lacquered skin in shifting shades of red.

Some of us have traveled a long distance to come to avenue d'Ivry. But most have only walked a couple of blocks. It is here, in the border land between the 13th and 14th arrondissements, that the lively Asian quarter extends. The patiently cooked Peking ducks are seen in many windows, but it is in Tang Frères' simple storefront that you find what is perhaps France's best. Also, hidden in one of the yard's run-down storehouse-like buildings is a gigantic food store where all the obligatory duck accompaniments can be bought: tender scallions, the best Hoisin sauce, and paper-thin pancakes. Making your own pancake-package with pieces of Peking duck, thin strips of cucumber and scallion and then dripping a little hoisin sauce on top is one of the tastiest and most pleasant food experiences on offer here.

The shops with their fluorescent lights are perhaps not the most charming of environments, but they give you the chance to study everyday Chinese life and to find many different products. How about "facing heaven", the famous chili from Sichuan? Or perhaps you'd prefer the number one ready-made meal from this part of the world—the myriad frozen dumplings with an array of fillings, ready for the steam cooker?

In a simple storefront on avenue d'Ivry you can find France's best Peking ducks

In the Asian quarter, both shops and restaurants are often small holes-in-the-wall, nooks where every square foot is used so that more items, another table, or a few chairs, can be squeezed in.

If you can't quite decide whether it was Sichuan heat or Cantonese specialities you wanted, this is definitely the right quarter to go to. But the neighborhood is not just Chinese; there are all East Asian peoples—and cuisines. Here you have the light, very fresh Vietnamese food where the fermented fish sauce *nuoc cham*, fresh herbs, and tons of chilies set their mark. But look out—even experienced chili-eaters like me begin to cold—sweat at the fiercest offerings; when the overpowering sensation has yielded, there'll be an adrenaline kick to really get you going.

If you haven't tried Cambodian food before, you've also come to the right place; Thai and Burmese—everything is represented here with good, simple restaurants and many food shops and kitchen stores.

The ethnic range of products is huge in this vibrant quarter, as is that of the prices and quality. You can spend all your holiday funds on the coveted seafood abalone, or on a few grams of an aphrodisiac in powdered form, carefully weighed in a Chinese pharmacy. If you want, an evening long dinner can be served in a private room, crowned by Chairman Mao's favourite sweet-and-sour pork.

In contrast, there are also gigantic restaurants where Chinese families, students, and tourists are quickly served three-course meals for 7 dollars. These meals can end with flambéed pineapple, where the fruit ends up on a tea saucer, cognac is poured over it, and then a cigarette lighter is used to set it on fire, right in front of you.

SENCHA MARTINI

Green tea and cilantro martini

1 SHOT GIN
1 OZ BREWED SENCHA TEA, cold
8 CILANTRO LEAVES
4 LONG, THIN CUCUMBER STRIPS

Mix together the gin, tea, and cilantro. Distribute the cucumber among 4 frozen glasses. Pour the gin tea into the glasses.

☞ *Sencha is Japan's favorite kind of tea.*

CURRY VERT

Green curry paste

14 GREEN CHILIES

5 GARLIC CLOVES

3 SHALLOTS, finely chopped

1 TBSP LEMON GRASS, thinly sliced

1 TBSP GINGER, coarsely chopped

1 LIME, grated peel and juice

3 LIME LEAVES, finely chopped

1 BUNCH CILANTRO, chopped

¼ TSP ASIAN SHRIMP PASTE, available in Asian stores

½ TSP GROUND CUMIN

½ TSP CORIANDER

½ TBSP FISH SAUCE

1. Place all the ingredients in a food processor and add 4–5 tbsp water. Blend to a smooth paste.
2. Store the curry paste in a jar with a tight-fitting cover in the refrigerator.

☞ *This is a recipe I like, but the recipe for curry mixtures varies depending on whom you ask. In Thailand, every family has its own variation of this spice mix. If you make the recipe once, you can easily change it according to your taste. The point of a spice paste is to avoid buying a thousand spices each time you make food. You make this once in a while, store it in the refrigerator, and use it as you would a stock cube.*

NEMS VIETNAMIENS

Vietnamese spring rolls

4 RICE PAPERS, soaked in lukewarm water
½ CARROT, in thin strips
1 RED CHILI, in strips
2 SCALLIONS, sliced lengthwise
¼ ICEBERG LETTUCE HEAD, shredded
3 ½ OZ PEELED SHRIMP
4 TSP FRESH MINT
4 TSP CILANTRO

DIP SAUCE
2 OZ SUGAR
½ C RICE VINEGAR
2 TBSP FISH SAUCE
1 TSP THAI CHILI, finely chopped
3 TBSP GRATED DAIKON
1 ½ OZ UNSALTED PEANUTS, chopped
1 SCALLION, thinly sliced
2 TBSP CILANTRO, coarsely chopped
1 TBSP MINT, coarsely chopped

1. Set out the soaked rice papers. Arrange the carrot, chili, scallions, and iceberg lettuce in the middle of each. Distribute the shrimp and top with 1 tsp mint and 1 tsp cilantro. Roll together and cover the rolls with a wet towel so they do not dry out.

2. Boil the sugar with ½ c water. Cool. Add the rest of the ingredients for the dip sauce and serve the sauce with the shrimp rolls.

ŒUFS PÉKINOIS

Soy eggs

4 EGGS
⅔ C LIGHT SOY SAUCE
2 TBSP DARK SOY SAUCE
3 OZ SUGAR
ABOUT 1 IN GINGER, thinly sliced

1. Boil the eggs for 6 minutes. Wash them in cold water and peel.
2. Place the rest of the ingredients in a saucepan, add ⅔ c water, and boil. Lower the heat to the lowest setting and add the eggs. Stir them around at regular intervals. Cool the eggs in the liquid. Serve as they are, cold and in the liquid.

ŒUFS CROUSTILLANTS

Fried eggs in ginger stock

4 EGGS

¼ C RICE VINEGAR

½ TSP SALT

2 TBSP SUGAR

2 TBSP DRY SHERRY

1 TBSP LIGHT SOY SAUCE

1 TBSP GINGER, grated

CORN OIL, for frying

3 SCALLIONS, sliced into long thin strips

½ CARROT, in thin strips

1 RED CHILI, shredded

4 TSP CILANTRO

1. Boil the eggs for 4 minutes. Cool down in cold water and peel. Place on paper towels and dry.
2. Heat the vinegar, salt, sugar, sherry, soy sauce, and ginger in a saucepan over low heat until the sugar has melted.
3. Heat the oil to 350°F (180°C). Lower the eggs into the oil using a perforated ladle and fry them until they are golden-brown. Drain on paper towels.
4. Serve the eggs with the boiled, warm liquid, the vegetables and the cilantro.

GAMBAS SHANGHAI
Shrimp dumplings with chili and cilantro

16 WONTON WRAPPERS, available in Asian stores

FILLING

9 SHRIMP, peeled and chopped

1 TBSP CILANTRO, finely chopped

1 TBSP SCALLION, finely chopped

1 ½ TSP GRATED GINGER

1 TSP SAKE

1 TSP SOY SAUCE

1 TSP OYSTER SAUCE

¼ TSP SUGAR

¼ TSP SESAME OIL

STOCK

2 ½ C CHICKEN STOCK

2 LEMON GRASS STALKS, crushed

3 GARLIC CLOVES, crushed

1 THAI CHILI, finely chopped

1 TBSP GINGER, thinly sliced

4 SMALL BOK CHOY, quartered

3 SCALLIONS, thinly sliced

2 TBSP WHOLE CILANTRO LEAVES

4 TSP FRESH THAI BASIL

1 ½ TBSP SOY SAUCE

1 TBSP FISH SAUCE

½ TSP SESAME OIL

1. Mix all the ingredients for the filling. Place 2 piles of filling on 8 of the wonton wrappers. Brush the edges with water and place the rest of the wrappers on top. Press the dough around the piles of filling. Slice apart the dough between the pillows.
2. Boil the chicken stock together with the lemon grass, garlic, chili, and ginger. Remove from the heat and leave, covered, for 30 minutes.
3. Strain the stock. Boil the dumplings in the stock for about 2 minutes. Add the rest of the ingredients. Boil and season, as desired, with more sesame oil and fish sauce.

Along avenue d'Ivry, there are many Asian shops and hole-in-the-wall restaurants.

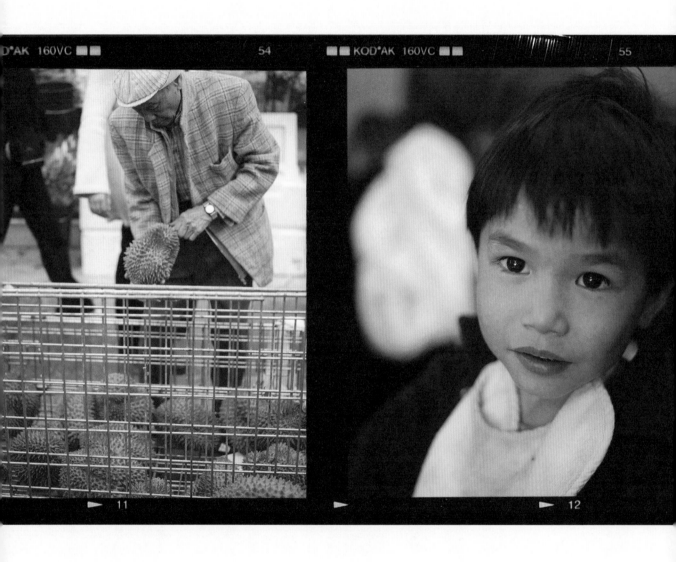

BARBECUE DE SAUMON CHINOIS

Barbecue salmon with Chinese spices

1 LB SALMON FILLET

¼ C HONEY

4 TBSP SOY SAUCE

2 TBSP SAKE

2 TBSP GINGER, grated

1 TBSP OYSTER SAUCE

2 TSP FIVE-SPICE, see recipe below

½ TSP SESAME OIL

1. Place all the ingredients except for the salmon in a saucepan and simmer over low heat for 10 minutes. Cool.
2. Separate the salmon lengthwise and place in the marinade. Put on a plate, cover with plastic wrap, and put in the refrigerator overnight.
3. Scrape any extra marinade off the salmon. Fry the salmon for about 30 seconds on each side over high heat. Cool.
4. Thinly slice the salmon and serve with a green salad.

FIVE-SPICE

2 TBSP CRUSHED CINNAMON STICK

2 TBSP GROUND GINGER

2 STAR ANISE

2 TBSP FENNEL SEEDS

2 TBSP CLOVES

Grind all the ingredients to a powder in a spice or coffee grinder. Store the spice mixture in a jar with a tight-fitting cover. Good for marinating light meat or fish before grilling.

SANDRE DES ÎLES
Thai pikeperch chowder

2 LB PIKEPERCH, skin-free, cut into ¾ in cubes

3 TBSP OIL

4 POTATOES, peeled and cubed

6 OZ JASMINE RICE

1 ONION, peeled and in strips

2 GARLIC CLOVES, finely chopped

2 IN GINGER, shredded

2 CARROTS, peeled and cubed

1 GREEN CHILI, chopped

1 ½ TBSP GREEN CURRY PASTE, see recipe page 234

6 C CHICKEN STOCK

2 ½ C COCONUT MILK

3 ½ OZ SHIITAKE MUSHROOMS, coarsely sliced

4 LIME LEAVES

2 LEMON GRASS STALKS, finely chopped

3 TSP FISH SAUCE

2 SCALLIONS, finely sliced

3 TSP CILANTRO, coarsely chopped

4 LIMES, juice

¼ C SOY SAUCE

1. Heat the oil in a frying pan. Add the potatoes, uncooked rice, onion, garlic, ginger, carrots, chili, and curry paste and cook for 5 minutes over high heat while stirring. Add the stock and coconut milk. Simmer for 20 minutes.
2. Add the mushrooms, lime leaves, lemon grass, and fish sauce. Stir, remove from heat, and leave, covered, for 20 minutes.
3. Warm the soup just before serving. Add the fish pieces. Simmer for 2 minutes. Finish by adding the scallion, cilantro, lime juice, and soy sauce.

☞ *Little Pho Banh-Cuon is one of the Asian quarter's most visited soup restaurants. That's where I first tried this soup.*

POULET AU SÉSAME
Sesame chicken with cucumber salad

4 CHICKEN THIGHS
CORN OIL, for frying

SESAME SAUCE

3 TBSP CASHEW NUTS, roasted
2 GARLIC CLOVES
2 OZ SUGAR
1 ½ IN PIECE FRESH ROOT GINGER
¼ C SOY SAUCE
¼ C SESAME OIL
¼ C TOMATO PURÉE
¼ C RICE VINEGAR
1 TSP MUSTARD POWDER
2 TBSP SESAME SEEDS, roasted
¼ C COCONUT MILK
3 DROPS TABASCO
¼ C CHICKEN STOCK

CUCUMBER SALAD

1 CUCUMBER, thinly sliced
1 RED CHILI, finely chopped
2 SCALLIONS, finely chopped
1 BUNCH CILANTRO, finely chopped
1 TBSP RICE VINEGAR
SALT AND BLACK PEPPER

1. Score each chicken thigh with a sharp knife. Brown them in the corn oil in a frying pan.
2. Blend all the ingredients for the sesame sauce together.
3. Coat the chicken thighs in the sesame sauce and place in a baking dish. Bake in the oven at 300°F (150°C) for about 10 minutes. Place the extra sauce to the side.
4. Mix the vegetables for the salad with the vinegar, salt, and pepper. Serve the chicken with the salad. Top with some chopped cashews and the rest of the sauce.

PORC CROUSTILLANT AIGRE-DOUX

Crispy pork with sweet~and~sour vegetables

1 LB PORK LOIN, in slices ¾ in thin

1 ½ TBSP + 1 ½ OZ CORN FLOUR

2 EGG YOLKS, lightly beaten

3 TSP SOY SAUCE

2 TSP SESAME OIL

1 TSP SALT

1 OZ FLOUR

CORN OIL, for frying

SWEET-AND-SOUR SAUCE

5 TBSP SAKE

1 TSP SALT

4 TBSP SUGAR

4 GARLIC CLOVES, crushed

2 TBSP GINGER, grated

¼ PINEAPPLE, peeled and cut into
smaller pieces

1 RED CHILI, cut into slices

1 CARROT, peeled and thinly sliced

1 SMALL CUCUMBER, peeled and chopped

½ YELLOW PEPPER, cut into strips

2 TOMATOES, thinly sliced

2 TBSP SOY SAUCE

¼ C RICE VINEGAR

1. Dissolve 1 ½ tbsp corn flour in 1 tbsp cold water in a bowl. Add the egg yolks, soy sauce, sesame oil, and salt. Place the pork loin in the marinade. Cover the bowl with plastic wrap and let sit in the refrigerator overnight.
2. Warm the sake, salt, and sugar for the sauce in a pot until the sugar has melted. Add the garlic and ginger and simmer over low heat for 5 minutes. Add the pineapple, chili, carrot, cucumber, pepper, and tomatoes. Simmer for 3 more minutes. Turn off the heat and add soy sauce and rice vinegar.
3. Mix the flour with 1 ½ oz corn flour. Take the meat out of the marinade and roll it in the flour mixture. Heat the oil to 350°F(180°C) in a heavy-based pan. Fry the pork slices until golden brown and drain on paper towels. Serve with the sweet-and-sour sauce and rice.

SAUCE TAMARIN AIGRE-DOUCE

Tamarind and soy sauce glaze

½ C CHICKEN STOCK
2 TBSP RICE VINEGAR
2 LEMON GRASS, thinly chopped
1 TBSP GRATED ORANGE PEEL
2 TBSP TAMARIND PURÉE
¼ C SOY SAUCE
2 TBSP DARK SYRUP
2 TBSP BROWN SUGAR
2 TBSP GARLIC, crushed
2 TBSP GINGER, grated
2 TBSP CHILI SAUCE

Mix all the ingredients in a pot and simmer over low heat for 10–15 minutes. Blend with a handheld mixer. Strain.

☞ *A tamarind looks like a big peanut but has a sweet-and-sour flavor that adds a fresh note to heavy casseroles and sauces.*

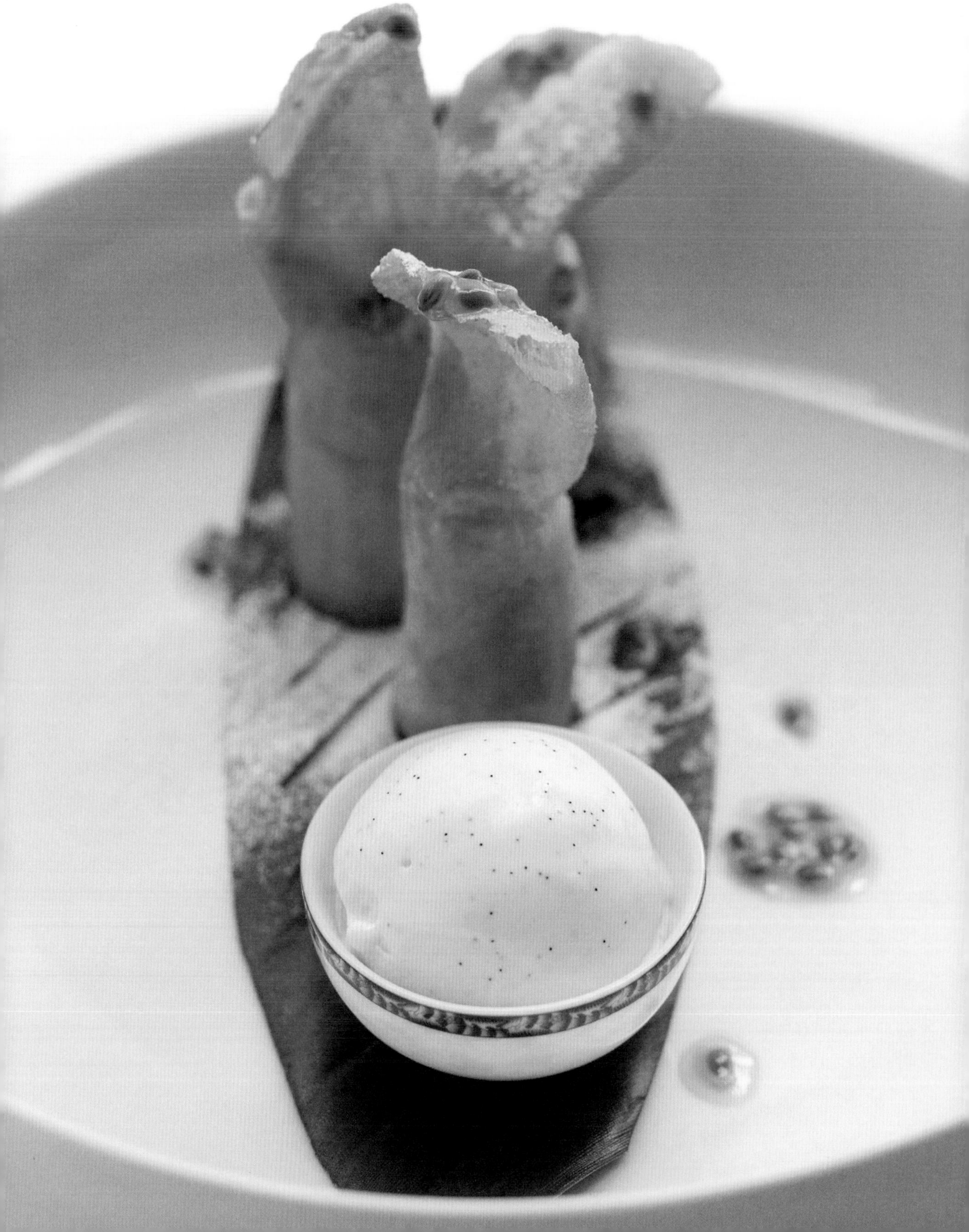

BANANES FRITES AU FRUIT DE LA PASSION

Fried bananas with passion fruit

4 BANANAS, cut into 3 pieces each

3 SHEETS BRICK DOUGH (a type of filo dough)

2 EGG YOLKS, for brushing

¼ C PASSION FRUIT SEEDS

¼ C ORANGE FLOWER HONEY

2 TBSP LIME JUICE

CORN OIL, for frying

CONFECTIONERS' SUGAR

1. Cut the round dough sheets into quarters. Brush them with egg yolk and roll each banana piece in dough.
2. Mix the passion fruit and honey in a pot and quickly boil. Remove from the heat and add the lime juice.
3. Heat the oil to 350°F (180°C) and fry the bananas until golden-brown. Dust with confectioners' sugar and drip over the passion fruit honey. Serve with vanilla ice cream.

PARFAIT AU COCO ET AU CITRON VERT

Coconut and lime parfait with strawberries

⅔ C COCONUT LIQUEUR
3 LIMES, juice and grated peel
7 OZ SUGAR
8 EGG YOLKS
3 C WHIPPING CREAM
16 STRAWBERRIES, sliced
CONFECTIONERS' SUGAR

COCONUT CHIPS
1 COCONUT

1. Mix coconut liqueur, lime juice, and 5 ½ oz sugar in a stainless steel bowl. Add the egg yolks and whip to a stiff foam over a double boiler. Remove from heat and continue whipping until the mixture has cooled to room temperature.
2. Whip the cream lightly so that it flows thickly and add it to the egg mixture. Distribute the parfait among four 3 ½ in ramekins . Freeze.
3. Crush the coconut and remove the flesh. Slice thinly and place it on a tray. Dry it in the oven at 325°F(160°C) for about 7 minutes until the chips are golden-brown.
4. Mix 1 ½ oz sugar and 2 tbsp grated lime peel. Roll the parfaits in the mixture before serving them. Powder the strawberries with the rest of the mixture and place them on the parfaits. Top with the coconut chips and powder with confectioners' sugar.

All recipes are for 4 people, unless otherwise stated.

The variety of useful addresses in Paris is practically infinite. Below is listed a handful of streets where you will find restaurants, food stores, markets, and small shops.

LA GOUTTE D'OR – *The African Quarter*
18:e arr. MÉTRO: Chateau Rouge

Rue Doudeauville
Rue Dejean
Rue Poulet
Rue des Poissonniers
Rue de Suez

BARBÈS – *The Arab Quarter*
18:e arr. MÉTRO: Barbès-Rochechouart

Boulevard Barbès
Boulevard de Rochechouart
Rue de Chartres
Rue de la Goutte d'Or
Rue Polonceau

LE MARAIS – *The Jewish Quarter*
4:e arr. MÉTRO: Saint-Paul or Bastille

Rue des Rosiers
Rue des Francs Bourgeois
Rue du Roi de Sicile
Rue des Ecouffes
Rue Pavée
Place des Vosges

SAINT-MICHEL – *The Greek Quarter*
5:e arr. MÉTRO: Saint-Michel

Rue de la Huchette
Rue Saint Séverin
Rue de la Harpe
Rue Xavier Privas

LA CHAPELLE – *The Indian Quarter*
10:e arr. MÉTRO: La Chapelle

Rue du Faubourg Saint-Denis
Boulevard de la Chapelle
Rue Louis Blanc
Rue Philippe de Girard

LE TREIZIÈME – *The Asian Quarter*
13:e arr. MÉTRO: Place d'Italie or Tolbiac

Avenue d'Ivry
Avenue de Choisy
Rue de Tolbiac
Rue Baudricourt
Rue de la Pointe d'Ivry

TRADITIONAL MARKETS

Marché Bastille (Richard-Lenoir)
Boulevard Richard Lenoir between rue Amelot and rue Saint-Sabin
11:e arr. MÉTRO: Bastille
Thursday 7–14.30, Sunday 7–15.

Marché Maubert
Place Maubert
5:e arr. MÉTRO: Maubert – Mutualité
Tuesday and Thursday 7–14.30, Saturday 7–15.

Marché Saint-Honoré
Place du Marché Saint-Honoré
1:a arr. MÉTRO: Pyramides
Wednesday 15–20.30, Saturday 7–15.

Marché des Enfants rouges
39 rue de Bretagne
3:e arr. MÉTRO: Filles du Calvaire
Tuesday–Thursday 8.30–13 and 16–19.30,
Friday–Saturday 8.30–13 and 16–20,
Sunday 8–14.

Marché Beauvau
Place d'Aligre
12:e arr. MÉTRO: Ledru-Rollin
Tuesday–Saturday 8.30–13 and 16–19.30,
Sunday 8.30–13.30.